A Faith Worth Believing

Kenneth Onstot

Eric, hope you enjoy
the book!

Ken

LUCAS PARK BOOKS

ST. LOUIS, MISSOURI

ISBN 9781603500722

Published by Lucas Park books
www.lucasparkbooks.com

Printed in the United States of America

Contents

Introduction

Choosing Faith

It was not the kind of conversation I expected to have in a high school lunch room. I was sitting across from Mike, my high school debate partner. Mike was bright, critical, and could smoke out a fraudulent piece of evidence or a logical error in the most polished speeches. But when it came to religion, Mike used the same intellectual and critical skills against my beliefs that he used against our opponents. So in the lunch room that day he said to me, "Do you believe in a loving God?"

I figured he was setting me up. "Yes," I said cautiously.

"Do you also admit that there is evil in the world?"

"Yes."

"Then if your God is loving, he must not be all powerful, and if he is all powerful he must not be loving."

This, of course, is a classic dilemma for the Christian faith, as well as other monotheistic religions. But it was a little unnerving to have it thrown at me by a high school classmate channeling Socrates.

Unfortunately Mike was so good at tearing down the faith of others, he had no faith of his own. He struggled with depression, some of which may have been biochemical, but some of which came from his inability to see any meaning in life. Mike viewed life much like Shakespeare's Macbeth:

Life's but a walking shadow, a poor player
That struts and frets his hour upon the stage
And then is heard no more: it is a tale
Told by an idiot, full of sound and fury
Signifying nothing.

One day I was riding with Mike in his car, and suddenly he said to me, "Why do you believe in God?" I answered, "Because I don't think we are alone in the world. I believe we were put here for a purpose and that we are loved." He was silent for a moment and then said, "I wish I could believe that."

I did not know what to say, so I let it go. But looking back at the conversation, I realized that Mike had given me a valuable insight. Even though I could not prove the truth of my faith, it was a faith worth believing.

The New Testament says, "Always be ready to make your defense to anyone who demands from you an accounting for the hope that is in you; yet do it with gentleness and reverence" (I Peter 3:15-16). This book is an accounting for hope. It is not apologetics as much as testimony. It is less a reasoned defense of the Christian faith than an invitation to share its hope. It is what I wish I could have said to Mike 40 years ago.

While thinking of non-believers, I also write this book for believers. Perhaps even more for believers. Christians also struggle, sometimes daily, with whether to believe what we have been taught about Jesus. I hope this book gives encouragement—a reason to believe even when we lack proof of those beliefs or answers to every question.

The Decision

Years after my conversation with Mike, I attended a lecture at Whitworth University given by Dallas Willard, who at the time was a professor of philosophy at the University of Southern California. He told of being asked by a colleague, "Why are you a follower of Jesus Christ?" He answered, "Whom else do you suggest?"

According to the Bible, the question is not whether we will believe in a god, but which one. After entering the Promised Land, Joshua issued this challenge to the people of Israel:

Now therefore revere the Lord, and serve him in sincerity and in faithfulness; put away the gods that your ancestors served beyond the River and in Egypt, and serve the Lord. Now if you are unwilling to serve the Lord, choose this day whom you will serve, whether the gods your ancestors served in the region beyond the River or the gods of the Amorites in whose land you are living; but as for me and my household, we will serve the Lord (Joshua 24:14-15).

Joshua did not attempt a philosophical argument for committing one's life to the Lord; he asked the Israelites to make a choice.

Similarly, when Elijah challenged the people of Israel on Mt. Carmel, he said, "How long will you go limping with two different opinions? If the Lord is God, follow him, but if Baal, then follow him" (I Kings 18:21). Centuries later when Jesus called his first disciples, he said to them, "Follow me." He did not argue with them; he summoned them to make a choice. It is true that later Jesus said to them, "You did not choose me, but I chose you" (John 15:16). We will look at the dynamics of choosing and being chosen in chapter 5. But Jesus did not engage his first disciples in apologetics; he invited them to make a commitment.

In his *Large Catechism* Martin Luther writes,

A god is that to which we look for all good and in which we find refuge in every time of need. To have a god is nothing else than to trust and believe in [that god] with our whole heart. As I have often said, the trust and faith of the heart alone make both God and an idol.[1]

By that definition everyone has a god. All people have someone or something on which they place their trust or to which they commit their hope. It may be a goal, job, relationship, organization, hobby, recreation, or addiction. It may involve transcendent beings or human ones. If we have no other god, we will probably make ourselves into one.

The Consequences of Our Choice of Gods

While in college I took my first philosophy class: an introduction to existentialism. There I was introduced to Friedrich Nietzsche, champion of a philosophy in which God is replaced by human self-determination, free from any transcendent religion. He was like an evangelist for atheism, more passionate about it even than my friend Mike.

In one of his books Nietzsche articulates his philosophy through a character named Zarathustra. Zarathustra has spent 10 years of solitude in the mountains and has now come down to give human beings the gift of knowledge. His message is that God is dead and that humans can now live free from the restrictions of God's commandments and the fear of God's judgment. They can learn to treasure this life, instead of sacrificing themselves for a non-existent future one. Zarathustra says,

> I beseech you, my brothers, *remain faithful to the earth*, and do not believe those who speak to you of otherworldly hopes! Poison-mixers are they, whether they know it or not. Despisers of life are they, decaying and poisoned themselves, of whom the earth is weary: so let them go.[2]

Later in this book I will argue that belief in a future life can increase our commitment to this life, if we understand the future life in the right way. But Zarathustra thinks we must be liberated from belief in life after death in order to embrace life before death.

Later Zarathustra encounters some girls dancing in the woods. Seeing Zarathustra, they stop, fearing that Zarathustra will think that dancing is wrong. But Zarathustra says, "How could I, you lightfooted ones, be an enemy of godlike dances? Or of girls' feet with pretty ankles?" But when the dance is over he grows sad.

> "The sun has set long ago," he said at last; "the meadow is moist, a chill comes from the woods.

Something unknown is around and looks thoughtful.
What? Are you still alive, Zarathustra? Why? What
for? By what? Whither? Where? How? Is it not folly
still to be alive?"[3]

Even when Zarathustra embraces life, a shadow is cast
over his reverie by nagging questions: Why are we here? Is
there any purpose or meaning to our lives other than our
own self-gratification?

Toward the end of the story, Zarathustra meets an old
man with vacant eyes who speaks a poem as if speaking to
God:

What wouldst thou, waylayer, from me?
Thou lightning-shrouded one! Unknown one! Speak,
What wilt thou, unknown—god?
What? Ransom?
Why wilt thou ransom?
Demand much! Thus my pride advises.
And make thy speech short! That my other pride advises.
Hah, hah!
Me, thou wilt have? Me?
Me—entirely?

I was startled by the way Nietzsche here gives voice to
a central feature of the gospel: that God seeks a relationship
with us and will pay a price to make it possible. Following
Zarathustra's lead, the old man turns his back on this
possibility, but then he laments God's departure from his life:

Away!
He himself fled.
My last, only companion,
My great enemy,
My unknown,
My hangman-god.
No! Do come back
With all thy tortures!
To the last of all that are lonely,

Oh, come back!
All my tear-streams run
Their course to thee;
And my heart's final flame—
Flares up for thee!
Oh, come back,
My unknown God! My pain! My last—happiness.[4]

When the poem ends Zarathustra beats the old man for being an actor—an imposter who said things he did not really believe. But the man defends himself by suggesting that he was playing Zarathustra, giving voice to the suppressed questions and yearnings in Zarathustra's own heart.

While championing the death of God, Nietzsche gave me new insight into why my faith was worth believing. We can get rid of God and become our own gods. But when we do, what will we have left? Having freed himself from God's commandments and the fear of God's judgment, Zarathustra must now live without God's overriding mercy, grace, and love.

Reading this in my dorm room, I realized again how important to me was the feeling that God was part of my life, even if that entailed a sense of accountability to God— of being bound by God's intention for human life. I knew at that moment I would prefer a life of accountability to God to having no God at all.

Rejecting Good News

One of the last Japanese soldiers to surrender at the end of World War II was an army intelligence officer named Hiroo Ononda. In 1944 he was sent to the island of Lubang in the Philippines to spy on U.S. forces in the area. When the allies captured the island, most of the Japanese soldiers fled or were captured. But Ononda and three others managed to evade capture and hide in the jungle.

They continued hiding even after Japan surrendered in 1945. Leaflets were dropped from the air announcing that the war was over, but Ononda and his compatriots did not believe them. Even when announced by Japanese citizens on loudspeakers, they thought it was a trick. So they continued hiding. Eventually one of the group surrendered, and two others were killed, but Ononda continued hiding, foraging for food in the jungle or stealing it from local farmers. Finally in 1974 his former commanding officer came to the island and persuaded Ononda that the war was over and that he could come out of hiding and go home.[5]

The failure to believe Good News can leave us in bondage to bad news. The truth that God actually loves us and has the power to save our fallen world can set us free from fear, regret, or hopelessness; but only if we believe it.

The Faith of Puddleglum

One of my favorite stories comes from *The Silver Chair*, one of the *Chronicles of Narnia* by C. S. Lewis. Two children named Jill Pole and Eustace Scrubb, along with a marshwiggle named Puddleglum, set out to rescue the prince of Narnia from an underground prison where he is held by an evil queen of the underworld. The queen has no real power over the children. She cannot force them to stay in her underground prison. But she tries to trap them by convincing them that her underground world is the only *real* world, that there is no world above them with grass, trees, and sky, no real Narnia ruled by a great lion named Aslan, who is C. S. Lewis' symbol for Jesus. The queen says,

"Narnia? … There is no land called Narnia."

"Yes, there is though, Ma'am," said Puddleglum. …

"Indeed," said the Witch. "Tell me, I pray you, where that country is?"

"Up there," said Puddleglum, stoutly, pointing overhead. "I don't know exactly where."

"How?" said the Queen, with a kind of soft, musical laugh, "Is there a country up among the stones and mortar of the roof?"

At this point the children struggle for a way to prove to the queen—and to themselves perhaps—that there is a real world above her dark cave, a world of trees, grass, sun, moon, and Aslan. But when the children try to describe it, they are forced to use analogies from the queen's cave, comparing the sun to a lamp that hangs in the sky. The queen asks, "Hangs from what?" Then while they think how to answer, she says,

> "You see? When you try to think out clearly what this *sun* must be, you cannot tell me. You can only tell me it is like the lamp. Your *sun* is a dream; and there is nothing in the dream that was not copied from the lamp. The lamp is the real thing; the *sun* is but a tale, a children's story."[6]

Finally Puddleglum, the most pessimistic of the bunch, speaks up and says to the witch,

> "One word, Ma'am. ... Suppose we *have* only dreamed, or made up all those things—trees and grass and sun and moon and stars and Aslan himself. Suppose we have. Then all I can say is that, in that case, the made-up things seems a good deal more important than the real ones. Suppose this black pit of a kingdom of yours *is* the only world. Well, it strikes me as a pretty poor one. ... That's why I'm going to stand by the play world. I'm on Aslan's side even if there isn't any Aslan to lead it. I'm going to live as like a Narnian as I can even if there isn't any Narnia."[7]

Simon Weil once said, "The danger is not lest the soul should doubt whether there is any bread, but lest by a lie it should persuade itself that it is not hungry."[8]

Faith arises from a hunger within us, but that does not make it false. Sigmund Freud suggested that religion is a wish-fulfillment, a projection on to a cosmic canvas of our need for comfort in a threatening, hostile universe. But the fact that faith fills a need does not make it untrue, any more than oxygen is imaginary because it satisfies our need for breathing. It is not an argument against faith to say it gives our lives comfort and meaning. I would say it is an argument *for* faith.

Faith and Doubt

Because faith is ultimately a commitment, it is not immune to doubt. In Mark chapter 9, a desperate father came to Jesus asking healing for his son. He said to Jesus, "If you are able to do anything, have pity on us and help us." Jesus replied, "If you are able!—All things can be done for the one who believes." Immediately the father cried out, "I believe; help my unbelief" (Mark 9:22-24).

Many heroes of the Bible experienced a mixture of faith and doubt. Abraham believed the Lord, and the Lord reckoned it to him as righteousness (Genesis 15:6). But two chapters later when God tells Abraham that his 90 year-old wife Sarah will bear a son, Abraham laughs. On the cross Jesus says, "My God, my God, why have you forsaken me?" (Mark 15:34), echoing a psalm sung for centuries by people of faith (Psalm 22). Job acknowledges God's sovereignty (Job 1:21), then spends the next 30 chapters questioning God's fairness. Precisely because faith involves a relationship, it can also involve struggle.

After being a pastor for over 35 years and a believer in Jesus as long as I can remember, there are times when I still wonder if it is all true. How do I know there is a God out there, and if there is, how do I know God cares anything at all about tiny creatures in one lonely edge of the universe? Do I believe in a loving God so I will feel less alone or less afraid of death? Do I believe because my job depends on it, or my sense of self-worth? And how do I justify belief in a loving God when faced with the enormity of suffering in the world?

Faith does not mean being untroubled by doubt. The greatest barrier to faith is not doubt, but indecision. In Yann Martel's novel *Life of Pi*, a story rooted in issues about faith and decision, the narrator says,

It is not atheists who get stuck in my craw but agnostics. Doubt is useful for a while. We must all pass through the garden of Gethsemane. If Christ played with doubt, so must we. If Christ spent an anguished night in prayer, if he burst out from the cross, "My God, my God, why have you forsaken me?" then surely we are also permitted doubt. But we must move on. To choose doubt as a philosophy of life is akin to choosing immobility as a means of transportation.[9]

Even as a pastor, doubts periodically flow through my mind. But I keep coming back to the question of alternatives. Is life really full of sound and fury signifying nothing? Certainly there are non-religious people who find satisfaction in human relationships and a quiet joy in the sheer amazingness of life. But when I experience these things, I find welling up in me an emotion that can only be described as gratitude, and gratitude seeks someone to thank. It seeks a Giver. So even in the midst of doubt I find myself drawn back to faith. Again and again I choose to believe.

Can God be Proved?

It is said that love is blind, but must the same be true for faith? Many able philosophers have attempted proofs for the existence of God. The most common is the idea of a First Cause. Someone or something must have gotten the world started. Related to this is the argument by design. The universe as we know it is possible only because of finely balanced forces. For example, the universe as we know it would not exist without just the right balance between the forces pushing the universe apart and the force of gravity pulling it together. The balance in these forces, it is argued, could not have been the result of chance.

But these arguments tend to be more effective for people who already believe in God. Those who do not believe in God find other explanations.

In their book *The Grand Design*, Stephen Hawking and Leonard Mlodinow describe evidence that our universe is one of many universes that exist simultaneously, just as our solar system is one of many solar systems in the galaxy. This means that the cosmos had an almost infinite number of tries at producing the very universe we experience with just the right conditions for human life. The authors explain,

That means that in the same way that the environ-
mental coincidences of our solar system were rendered
unremarkable by the realization that billions of such
systems exist, the fine-tunings in the laws of nature
can be explained by the existence of multiple universes. Many people through the ages have attributed
to God the beauty and complexity of nature that in
their time seemed to have no scientific explanation.
But just as Darwin and Wallace explained how the
apparently miraculous design of living forms could
appear without intervention by a supreme being,
the multiverse concept can explain the fine-tuning of
physical law without the need for a benevolent creator
who made the universe for our benefit.[10]

I share this not to endorse their argument, nor to enter
into a debate about cosmology and evolution. My point is to
show how unlikely it is for a person like Stephen Hawking
to be convinced of God through scientific argument. It is
like using a scientific argument to propose marriage. The
decision must be made on other grounds.

Even if we argue for the existence of God based on a
First Cause or Intelligent Design, we would still be far from
understanding the nature of God. Is the universe the result of
warring gods as in the Babylonian myths, or an impersonal
Force like in *Star Wars*? Is God far removed from physical
life as in gnostic theology, or intimately involved in this
world in an ongoing way? The alternatives are not proven or
disproven scientifically, they are the premises on which one
chooses to base one's life, and the decision between them has
consequences for everything else in our lives.

The Consequences of Faith

This book, therefore, is not a proof for the Christian
faith, but a discussion of its consequences. The Bible not
only affirms that God exists; it emphasizes that God is
personal and desires a personal relationship with us. This
understanding of God and its implications is the subject of
chapter 1.

However, any belief in God must also deal with the problem of evil, as my debate partner Mike pointed out. And we must ask not only why evil exists but what God plans to do about it. More specifically we need to understand what it means that God intervenes in our world through a first century human being named Jesus. That is the subject of chapters 2–4.

But if our hope lies in God, what does this say about our purpose as human beings? How are we to live in light of God's actions and grace shown to us in Jesus, and what difference will that make in our still suffering world? These issues are addressed in chapters 5–9.

Finally in the last chapter we come to the question of how to believe. When my debate partner Mike says, "I wish I could believe that," is there any help to offer him?

Which Christian Faith?

Obviously the term "Christian faith" covers a wide variety of beliefs. Ultimately, this book represents my beliefs as a Christian. I do not claim to speak for the whole Christian church in all times and places. I am a Presbyterian pastor, and my particular beliefs are best described as North American mainline Protestant. I am aware that my particular cultural background shapes my understanding of what it means to be a follower of Jesus Christ. I also know that Christians in other times and places have described this differently.

Nevertheless, I think that most of the perspectives I share in this book will be recognizably Christian, especially when compared to their non-Christian alternatives. Such beliefs include:

1. That the world and its people were created by a personal God who communicates to human beings God's character and intentions, and who acts in human history past, present, and future.
2. That human beings have broken the relationship to God they were intended to have, and in the process have "broken" the creation, so that the world is not the place God wants it to be.

3. That to restore this broken relationship God came into the world personally in the human being Jesus of Nazareth, whose life, death, and resurrection show what God intends for human life and make that life possible.
4. That God's work will one day be finished in a new creation, a transformed heaven and earth in which God's intentions for human life and all creation will be fulfilled.
5. That the Bible is an authoritative source for us in understanding these beliefs.

This is not a complete list of Christian beliefs. In the pages that follow I will discuss many other matters such as grace, prayer, the church, mission, heaven, hell, Satan, and the kingdom of God. At no point do I claim to speak for all Christians, nor to cover all points of Christian doctrine. This book is not a systematic theology. It is a testimony—a personal account of the hope that is within me—presented, I pray, with gentleness and reverence.

1

It's Personal

I was 7 years old when I met my first theologian. She was my Vacation Bible School teacher at a small church in San Bernardino, CA. I don't remember her name; I knew her for only a week. A few months later the Air Force transferred my father to another base, and I never saw her again. But over half a century later I still remember her. She taught us stories about Jesus, always reminding us that Jesus wanted each of us to be his followers just like the first disciples, and that his care and love for us would last forever.

Though I did not understand everything she said, her words about Jesus resonated in the obvious affection and care she showed for each of us in her class. In one of the lessons we heard about Jesus calming the storm on the sea. We cut out figures of Jesus and the boat to paste into our Vacation Bible School books. I pasted the boat down on the page and then realized that Jesus was supposed to be inside the boat, which meant I should have pasted Jesus down first, then pasted the boat over his legs so it looked like he was standing in it.

I took my page over to the teacher and said, "I did it wrong." She looked at it and said, "Don't worry. It can be fixed." She told me, "Paste Jesus on the outside of the boat in the spot where he is supposed to be standing." So I did. Then she cut out a boat from the sample material in her teacher packet and gave it to me. "There," she said, "now, paste this second boat directly on top of the first boat, and it will look like Jesus is inside. In fact it will look better, because it will be three-dimensional."

I was awestruck by her brilliance. Although I had no words for it at the time, I received from her a powerful illustration of God's grace: God covering our mistakes and in the process causing us to turn out better than we ever imagined.

This Vacation Bible School teacher was one of many people who gave me the sense that God cared about me personally. At the top of that list was my mother. Because my father was in the Air Force, he was frequently away from home on overseas assignments. He was gone for over five of my first fifteen years of life. But my mother was always there.

One night I went to bed sick with what would turn out to be appendicitis. In the middle of the night I woke up needing to throw up, and when I sat up I discovered that my mother was sitting next to me, checking on me, worried that I might have something worse than a passing stomach flu. She even had a basin ready in case I needed to throw up. When I did not get better, she got me to the hospital, sat with me in the emergency room, and was the first person I saw when I woke up from surgery.

It's not that my mother was different from many other mothers who care for their children. It was the way she combined this care with all the Bible stories she read to me growing up, the prayers she said with me at bedtime, and the way she and my father took me to church wherever we lived and got involved in the church themselves, even knowing that we might be there for only a year and a half. It was the combination of care and faith that made God feel real to me.

Only years later when I was in college and seminary, did I begin to put words to the theology of a God who cared about me personally.

A Personal Relationship to God

In the first chapter of Genesis, God says,

> Let us make humankind in our image, according to our likeness; and let them have dominion over the

fish of the sea, and over the birds of the air, and over the cattle, and over all the wild animals of the earth, and over every creeping thing that creeps upon the earth. So God created humankind in his image, in the image of God he created them; male and female he created them (Genesis 1:26-27).

What does it mean to be created in the image of God? Bible interpreters have offered several possibilities:[1]

1. We are created to look like God. While obviously taking the word "image" too literally, this interpretation has one positive feature: it warns us against over-spiritualizing the meaning. Whatever it means to be created in the image of God applies to human beings as a whole: physically, mentally, and spiritually.
2. We are created with special capabilities that distinguish us from other creatures, such as free will, consciousness, self-awareness, or imagination. The danger here is reductionism. The more we discover about the capabilities of animals, the more limited will be the characteristics that make humans in the image of God.
3. We are meant to be God's representatives to the rest of creation. This is supported by ancient Middle Eastern texts which describe the king as God's representative to the world, calling the king God's "image." It also explains the "dominion" humans are given over the rest of creation in verses 28–30. This interpretation should not be taken to mean that humans have the right to do whatever they want with the creation. It means that humans have responsibility as stewards of God's creation. More about this in chapter 7.
4. We are created with enough likeness to God, so that we are capable of a relationship with God.

This last point is, I believe, key to what it means for humans to be created in the image of God. Claus Westermann concludes his long discussion of this issue with these words:

Seen from another point of view, the sentence means that the uniqueness of human beings consists in their being God's counterparts. The relationship to God is not something which is added to human existence; humans are created in such a way that their very existence is intended to be their relationship to God.[2]

We were made for a relationship with God and with the ability to share that relationship with others. In his autobiographical *Confessions*, St. Augustine says of human beings, "The thoughts of you stir him so deeply that he cannot be content unless he praises you, because you made us for yourself and our hearts find no peace until they rest in you."[3] We were created for a relationship with God, and we are incomplete without it. As the Westminster Shorter Catechism says, the purpose of human beings is "to glorify God and enjoy God forever."[4]

The Personal Nature of God

In a famous scene from the movie *The Godfather*, Michael Corleone sits with his brother and the family counselor planning to assassinate a rival crime boss. To justify the hit Michael Corleone says, "It's not personal, it's strictly business."

With God it is never just business; it is always personal. We see this in one of the more scandalous features of the Bible: the portrayal of God with strong human emotions.

On numerous occasions the Bible pictures God as angry:

- Moses says to the people of Israel: "But the Lord was angry with me on your account and would not heed me" (Deuteronomy 3:26).
- "Therefore the Lord was very angry with Israel and removed them out of his sight; none was left but the tribe of Judah alone" (II Kings 17:18).
- "O Lord of hosts how long will you be angry with your people's prayers?" (Psalm 80:4).

An even more striking emotion for a deity is jealousy:

- "You shall not bow down to them [other gods] or worship them; for I, the Lord your God, am a jealous God..." (Exodus 20:5).
- "For the Lord your God is a devouring fire, a jealous God" (Deuteronomy 4:24).
- "How long, O Lord? Will you be angry forever? Will your jealous wrath burn like fire?" (Psalm 79:5).

At other times God is described as grieved:

- "The LORD saw that the wickedness of humankind was great in the earth, and that every inclination of the thoughts of their hearts was only evil continually. And the LORD was sorry that he had made humankind on the earth, and it grieved him to his heart" (Genesis 6:5-6).
- "But they [the people of Israel] rebelled and grieved his holy spirit" (Isaiah 63:10).

Precisely because our relationship to God is personal, the Bible can describe God as jealous, angry, and grieved when people throw away their relationship to God for a lesser relationship.

But this is balanced by frequent mention of God's compassion:

- "As a father has compassion for his children, so the Lord has compassion for those who fear him" (Psalm 103:13).
- "But the Lord will have compassion on Jacob and will again choose Israel, and will set them in their own land..." (Isaiah 14:1).
- "And after I have plucked them up, I will again have compassion on them, and I will bring them again to their heritage and to their land, everyone of them" (Jeremiah 12:15).

But the most important characteristic ascribed to God in the Bible is love.

- "For God so loved the world that he gave his only Son..." (John 3:16)
- "But God proves his love for us in that while we were still sinners Christ died for us" (Romans 5:8).
- "In this is love, not that we loved God but that he loved us and sent his Son to be the atoning sacrifice for our sins" (I John 4:10).

One of the most powerful descriptions of a personal God is found in Hosea 11. It begins by describing how God brought the people of Israel out of slavery in Egypt: "When Israel was a child, I loved him, and out of Egypt I called my son" (Hosea 11:1).

The deliverance from Egypt was more than a liberation from injustice; it was the rescuing of a personal relationship. But like a rebellious teenager, Israel turned its back on this relationship. God says,

> The more I called them,
> the more they went from me;
> they kept sacrificing to the Baals,
> and offering incense to idols (Hosea 11:2).

What follows is a remarkably tender description of God's relationship to the people of Israel (here called Ephraim):

> Yet it was I who taught Ephraim to walk,
> I took them up in my arms;
> but they did not know that I healed them.
> I led them with cords of human kindness,
> with bands of love.
> I was to them like those
> who lift infants to their cheeks.
> I bent down to them and fed them (Hosea 11:3-4).

A relationship to God cannot get more personal than that. And yet there are consequences of their rejection of God. God says,

They shall return to the land of Egypt,
and Assyria shall be their king,
because they have refused to return to me.
The sword rages in their cities,
it consumes their oracle-priests,
and devours because of their schemes.
My people are bent on turning away from me.
To the Most High they call,
but he does not raise them up at all (Hosea 11:5-7).

As a young child, I remember my grandfather getting angry with me when I crossed the busy highway in front of his house without an adult or older sibling to go with me. I was surprised, because my grandfather had never gotten angry with me or spoken harshly to me before. It felt like my grandfather had suddenly turned against me. But he was angry because he feared the potentially devastating consequences of my actions.

So it was for God with the people of Israel. We will look further into the consequences of turning away from God in chapter 2.

But even then God did not give up on the people of Israel. God says,

How can I give you up, Ephraim?
How can I hand you over, O Israel? …
My heart recoils within me;
my compassion grows warm and tender.
I will not execute my fierce anger;
I will not again destroy Ephraim;
for I am God and no mortal,
the Holy One in your midst,
and I will not come in wrath (Hosea 11:8-9).

God has a change of heart! This may seem strange to say about a God who is unchanging, but when the Bible talks about the unchangeableness of God, it does so to emphasize the reliability of God's promises. Within those promises, however, God is not afraid to change plans in response to human actions. The Bible depicts a real relationship between God and people, even while insisting on God's ultimate sovereignty. More about this in chapter 5.

God in Person

For Christians the clinching argument for the personal nature of God comes in the New Testament. Echoing the story of Genesis, the gospel of John starts out, "In the beginning was the Word, and the Word was with God, and the Word was God" (John 1:1).

There are shelves of literature on what John means by "the Word," but in its simplest form it means the word spoken by God at the beginning of Genesis—the word by which God created the world. God said, "Let there be light," and there was light. The universe was created by the word God spoke.

But in the next verse this Word becomes a person: "He was in the beginning with God" (John 1:2). Then John takes this a step further in verses 10-11: "He was in the world, and the world came into being through him; yet the world did not know him. He came to what was his own, and his own people did not accept him." Suddenly we have left the story of creation and entered the world of human history, setting the stage for what John says in verse 14: "And the Word became flesh and lived among us, and we have seen his glory, the glory of a father's only son, full of grace and truth." Finally in verse 17 John says, "The law was indeed given through Moses; grace and truth came through Jesus Christ."

Note the string of identifications: the Word by which God created the world has become flesh, full of grace and truth, and now we see this grace and truth in an historical human being—Jesus of Nazareth.

John's gospel, like the other gospels, teems with personal, relational language. In chapter 4 we will look more closely at the whole story of Jesus' life, death, and resurrection, and how it plays into God's relationship with the world. But for now I simply note that when Jesus enters the picture, God becomes unmistakably personal.

Like Christians throughout history I have struggled to understand the relationship of God and Jesus. I discovered in seminary that the Bible itself struggles to describe this relationship:

- "No one has ever seen God. It is God the only Son, who is close to the Father's heart, who has made him known" (John 1:18)."
- "Let the same mind be in you that was in Christ Jesus, who, though he was in the form of God, did not regard equality with God as something to be exploited, but emptied himself, taking the form of a slave, being born in human likeness. And being found in human form, he humbled himself and became obedient to the point of death—even death on a cross" (Philippians 2:5-8).
- "For in him all the fullness of God was pleased to dwell, and through him God was pleased to reconcile to himself all things, whether on earth or in heaven, by making peace through the blood of his cross" (Colossians 1:19-20).

The first Christians used a variety of phrases trying to describe the relationship between God and Jesus:

- "the only Son, who is close to the Father's heart"
- "he was in the form of God, ... but emptied himself"
- "in him all the fullness of God was pleased to dwell"

Christians have tried to depict this relationship with concepts like "incarnation" and "the Trinity" (adding the Holy Spirit), but they have never found the perfect words. Christians do not believe in two gods or three gods, only one. And yet we believe that God came to us personally in Jesus, and that through Jesus, God wants to have a personal relationship with us. Explaining this has eluded the most sophisticated theologians, and yet Christians, myself included, have clung to this idea.

The Danger of Making God Personal

In her book *A History of God*, Karen Armstrong examines the imagery used in the Bible to describe God. She says,

> Beneath the mythological imagery, however, a quite distinctive conception of the ultimate reality was beginning to emerge in Israel: the experience with this God is an encounter with a person. Despite his terrifying otherness, Yahweh [the God of the Bible] can speak and Isaiah can answer. Again, this would have been inconceivable to the sages of the *Upanishads*, since the idea of having a dialogue or meeting with Brahman-Atman would be inappropriately anthropomorphic.[5]

Later in her book Armstrong registers concern about this personalization of God:

> Yet a personal God can become a grave liability. He can be a mere idol carved in our own image, a projection of our limited needs, fears and desires. We can assume that he loves what we love and hates what we hate, endorsing our prejudices instead of compelling us to transcend them.[6]

Armstrong prefers a more impersonal, mystical, almost pantheistic, image of God, picturing God as more like an all-encompassing ground-of-being which suffuses and animates the world, as a soul suffuses the body. Such an understanding of God, Armstrong claims, prevents God from being identified with any one person or group, stripping away their idolatrous claims to divine privilege.

But making God into a mystical impersonal force does not prevent people from claiming divine status for their own personal desires. If the divine light is inside us, where is the voice to stop us from doing whatever we want? It is the very *particularity* of God revealed in Jesus Christ that challenges any self-serving god we try to invent.

A Reason for the Trinity

For a book called *The Spiritual Life of Children*, Robert Coles, a Harvard researcher, interviewed children from all over the world about their concepts of God. In some cases he asked them to draw pictures of God. He writes,

> Often children give God their own hair color; indeed, a blond Lord, a blond Jesus, give way to darker divinities as one moves from Sweden to Hungary and Italy, thence across the Mediterranean. ... The same thing happens with the eyes—a preponderance of blue eyes in the drawings of Swedish children yields southward to brown and dark eyes. In North and South America a similar pattern holds.[7]

This illustrates Karen Armstrong's concern about the personalization of God. When people picture God as a person, they tend to picture God to look like themselves. In the worst cases, they then use their picture of God to put down those who look different.

One day while Robert Coles was sitting with a group of children looking at drawings of God, a girl named Betsy held up the drawing of a 10 year-old boy named Hal. She questioned the drawing, pointing out that Hal gave God the same color of eyes and hair as Hal. Hal defended himself. "No one has ever seen God," he said, "not before you die. So how can you know?" Then he pointed at the stack of drawings and said, "There's no correct answer—they're all right. You see God, and I see Him, and He's how He looks to you and how He looks to me. He's both."[8]

In a way Hal is arguing for Karen Armstrong's vague, mystical understanding of God. But that does not really solve the problem. If everyone pictures God the way each person wants, there is no basis for challenging anyone's picture of God.

Another child in Robert Coles' group was an 11 year-old from Puerto Rico. He noticed that none of the other pictures drawn by the children at his Irish Catholic school looked like him. He said to Robert Coles, "The priests here treat us [Spanish speaking children from Puerto Rico] like we're not as good as they are, their people. To them, Jesus must be Irish! They'd tell you—they'd draw Him as if he has the same color hair they have, the same eyes."[9]

When people picture God any way they want, they often end up picturing God like themselves. Then they use that picture of God to put down people who are different.

Which is why I believe in the Trinity. The Trinity reveals a particular God with particular characteristics that cannot be made into any kind of God we want.

The word "Trinity" never occurs in the Bible, but there are many places in the Bible where the Trinity shows up. One is in Luke chapter 10. In verse 21 Jesus rejoices in the Holy Spirit that the hidden God has been revealed, not to the wise and intelligent but to infants, meaning to his disciples. Then in verse 22 he says, "All things have been handed over to me by my Father; and no one knows who the Son is except the Father, or who the Father is except the Son and anyone to whom the Son chooses to reveal him." It is God the Son—Jesus—who reveals to us God the Creator, a God who is, in a sense, hidden from us.

When picturing the Trinity, I tend to picture God the Father as a cloud. God the Creator is at least partially hidden from us behind the creation. We can learn certain things about God from nature. The universe certainly shows us how big and powerful God must be. But nature can be deceptive. The same natural forces that produce beautiful sunsets also give us terrifying volcanoes, devastating earthquakes, and frightening hurricanes, not to mention drought, cancer, and Ebola epidemics. Nature is ambiguous. From looking at nature you might just as easily assume that God is a capricious tyrant, like the gods of Greek mythology.

But the Son shows us what the Father is like. As the gospel of John says, "No one has ever seen God. It is God the only Son, who is close to the Father's heart who has made him known" (John 1:18). We know that God loves us, not from looking at a sunset or volcano, but from looking at Jesus. We know that God forgives us, because Jesus forgave us. We know that God cares for the poor, because Jesus cared for the poor. We know that God has a future for us, because God raised Jesus from the dead and promises to raise us up to be with him.

A comedy show from the 1970s called *All in the Family* featured a blue collar, beer drinking, blatantly prejudiced New Yorker named Archie Bunker. In one episode Archie launches into his usual tirade against blacks, Jews, and Polish people. Finally his Polish son-in-law has had enough. He says, "Just remember, Archie, Jesus was a Jew." Archie turns red and says, "What are you talking about? Jesus was no Jew. Jesus was as good a Christian as I am."

That's what Karen Armstrong fears: a personal god made into our own image. But a personal God who actually enters history and has a particular identity cannot be made into anything we want. The undeniable fact is that Jesus was Jewish! He never says or does anything to disavow that identity. The very Jesus whom Archie Bunker claims to worship exposes the lie in anti-Semitism. God cannot be anti-Jewish if God came into the world as a Jew. Other details in Jesus' life challenge other forms of self-serving idolatry. Jesus' words about the poor expose the lie that God favors the rich. His crucifixion exposes the lie that the kingdom of God can be won by violence. His command to make disciples of all nations forever excludes the lie that any one nation, race, or ethnic group is God's favorite. To be sure, there are Christians throughout history who have taught racism, militarism, or anti-Semitism. But they did so by ignoring what the Bible actually said about Jesus.

In the story of Jesus, we discover God's heart. When Jesus forgave people, he embodied God's mercy. When Jesus fed people, he embodied God's desire that all would have enough to eat. When Jesus healed people, he revealed God's intention that all people would be made whole. And when he welcomed Pharisees and tax collectors to his table, he made it clear that God wants all of us—rich and poor, respected and despised—to come to the banquet in his kingdom. Admittedly, throughout history Christians have lived contrary to these principles, but they have done so by selectively or totally ignoring what Jesus actually said and did.

But where does the Holy Spirit fit in? If Jesus shows us what God is like, then the Holy Spirit is the power and presence of God today showing us what Jesus is like. Jesus lived 2000 years ago. He died, rose from the dead, and ascended into heaven long before any of us were born. None of us living today have seen Jesus. But we have learned about Jesus from the Holy Spirit working through those who have passed on his words and actions.

It began when the Holy Spirit came upon the apostles at Pentecost. It continued as they started churches and wrote down the words and actions of Jesus in the Bible. It continues today in the people who have translated the Bible so we can read it in our own language and in faithful pastors and teachers who have taught the Bible.

I will say more about the Bible in a moment. But first one more note about the Holy Spirit. The Holy Spirit also tells that God is not male. The language of God the Father and God the Son can be misunderstood to mean that God is male and that, therefore, males are more like God than females. Admittedly, things get awkward here, because Jesus was male. To be a real human being he had to have a gender. But that does not mean God is male, any more than God is Middle Eastern because Jesus was born in Bethlehem. The Holy Spirit is a corrective in that regard. The Holy Spirit is not male or female. The term in Greek is neuter. But the Holy Spirit works through both males and females to show us what God is like. Thus at Pentecost we are told that the Holy Spirit came upon both men and women in that upper room.

The same is true of nationality. Jesus does not mean that God is more Middle Eastern than African, Asian, or European. The Holy Spirit showed that at Pentecost. At Pentecost the Holy Spirit spoke the languages of people from all races, nations, and languages to tell us about Jesus. Jesus shows us what God is like, and the Holy Spirit works through men and women of all nations to show us what Jesus is like.

Near the end of Matthew's gospel Jesus says, "Go therefore and make disciples of all nations, baptizing them in the name [singular!] of the Father and of the Son and of the Holy Spirit" (Matthew 28:19). One name, three persons.

As Christians we do not worship three gods, we worship one God, revealed to us in the Creator who gave us the world, the Savior who died for us on a cross, and the Spirit who works in our lives today. That is the blessing we are given in baptism, a blessing that prevents or at least restrains us from making God into our own image.

The Bible's Role in Understanding a Personal God

On November 13, 1934, a German professor of religion named Dr. Reinhold Krause addressed a rally of 20,000 German Christians at the Sports Palace in Berlin. He stated his belief that the German Reformation, begun by Martin Luther, would be completed in Hitler's Third Reich. According to Krause, the first step in the creation of this new German national church was to get rid of the Old Testament, purging the Bible of its talk about Jews being God's chosen people. But the New Testament also needed editing, he said, eliminating the idea that all of us are sinners and that Jesus had to die on a cross to forgive us. All that "superstitious nonsense" was to be torn out of the Bible, so that we would be left with a heroic Jesus, using his power to inaugurate a new kingdom that would last a thousand years—a *Reich*.[10]

Here we have another example of what Karen Armstrong fears: people using Jesus to promote idolatrous ideas. But notice that this is possible only by pruning the Bible's depiction of Jesus, selecting from the Bible's testimony only those parts that fit Nazi ideology.

Most are not as blatant as Reinhold Krause. But the same strategy—focusing on some parts of the story of Jesus while ignoring others—is used to make Jesus a proponent of slavery, white supremacy, American superiority, or God-promised prosperity. He is made into an idol by the selective reading of the Bible's testimony to him.

During my years growing up I did not understand the full significance of the Bible to our faith in Jesus. Initially for me the Bible was simply a source of stories about Jesus, which is still its most important function. But in college and seminary I began to realize that the Bible was also a firewall against idolatry. There is an ingrained tendency in us to create God in our own image, instead of letting God create us in God's image. The solution to this problem is not to get rid of the Bible, any more than to get rid of Jesus. The solution is to read the Bible *as a whole* keeping in mind the entire story of God and Jesus, not just those parts we can use to justify our self-interest. It is this desire to understand Jesus in light of the whole Bible that has motivated my preaching and teaching throughout my ministry.[11]

Changing Our Understanding of Prayer

As I have grown in my appreciation of a personal relationship to God, I have also received a new understanding of prayer.

Early in Mark Twain's novel *Huckleberry Finn*, Miss Watson tries to teach Huck Finn about prayer. Huck says,

Then Miss Watson she took me in the closet and prayed, but nothing came of it. She told me to pray every day, and whatever I asked for I would get it. But it warn't so. I tried it. Once I got a fish-line, but no hooks. It warn't any good to me without hooks. I tried for the hooks three or four times, but somehow I couldn't make it work. By and by, one day, I asked Miss Watson to try for me, but she said I was a fool. She never told me why, and I couldn't make it out no way.

I set down one time back in the woods, and had a long think about it. I says to myself, if a body can get anything they pray for, why don't Deacon Winn get back the money he lost on pork? Why can't the widow get back her silver snuff-box that was stole? Why can't Miss Watson fat up? No, says I to myself, there ain't nothing in it.[12]

If we see prayer only as a way to get things from God, then prayer will inevitably let us down, and we will miss its true purpose. But if we understand the purpose of our lives in terms of our relationship to God, prayer becomes essential to being human. It is not the results of prayer but the very act of prayer that reveals God's work in our lives.

Over the course of my life I have prayed for many things, such as healing when I went into surgery for my appendicitis. Sometimes I got what I prayed for, and sometimes I didn't. But as I got older I prayed less for God to give me something and more that God would be with me through something. I learned that what I needed was not some special blessing from God but God's presence in my life.

Frederick Buechner describes prayer this way:

> Just keep praying, Jesus says, … keep on beating the path to God's door, because the one thing you can be sure of is that down the path you beat with even your most half-cocked and halting prayer the God you call upon will finally come, and even if he does not bring you the answer you want, he will bring you himself. And maybe at the secret heart of all our prayers that is what we are really praying for.[13]

Prayer is not about getting what we want but about building the relationship with God for which we were made.

Changing Our Understanding of Heaven

Believing in a personal God who desires a personal relationship with us has also changed the way I view heaven.

Many books have been written by people who believe they have gone to heaven and come back. *Heaven is for Real*, by Todd Burpo, is the story of his three year-old son Colton who almost died during surgery for a ruptured appendix and who came back to tell about seeing Jesus and children with wings and a great grandfather whom he had never met. Todd concludes from his son's description that heaven is real.

A more sophisticated approach is offered in *Proof of Heaven*, by a neurosurgeon named Eben Alexander. Alexander was in a coma for seven days. Brain scans indicated that the neocortex of his brain had completely shut down. Yet when he recovered, Alexander could remember having experiences during this time period. He remembered rising through an opening of white light into a world where he was flying over a lush green countryside. Hundreds of people have reported visions like this during near death experiences.

I don't question these experiences, but I note that they are surprisingly absent from the teachings of Jesus. Particularly in the gospel of John, Jesus describes heaven in a different way than I had learned to think about it. In John's gospel heaven is not so much a place as a relationship.

We see Jesus moving in this direction during his conversation with the disciples on the night before his crucifixion. In John 14:2 he says to them, "In my Father's house there are many dwelling places. If it were not so, would I have told you that I go to prepare a place for you?" Here Jesus makes heaven sound like a place where he is preparing us a room. But in the next verse he says, "And if I go and prepare a place for you, I will come again and will take you to myself, so that where I am you may be also." Jesus begins by talking about a place, but ends up talking about a relationship: "You will be with me."

Thomas, as so often happens in John's gospel, misunderstands. He says to Jesus, "Lord, we don't know where you are going. How can we know the way?" Thomas thinks of heaven as a place you go, like Disney World. But Jesus replies, "I am the way, and the truth, and the life. No one comes to the Father except through me."

When Jesus says, "I am the way," he does not mean that he is the way to get where you want to go. He means that he himself is where you want to go. Heaven means being with Jesus, because when you are with Jesus you are with God.

The statement "In my Father's house are many dwelling places" contains an unusual Greek word. It is used only one other time in the New Testament: in the same chapter—John

14:23—where Jesus says, "Those who love me will keep my word, and my Father will love them, and we will come to them and make our home with them." The expression "make our home with them" uses the same Greek word as "dwelling places." In verse 2 Jesus says that in his Father's house are many dwelling places, but in verse 23 he says that he and God will make their dwelling place with us.

Which explains why Jesus says, "I am the way." He does not mean that he is the way to someplace else. He is the way because he is the destination. Jesus can take you where you want to go, because *he* is where you want to go. Heaven is not so much a place as a relationship.

Now let me qualify this. There are many passages in the Bible where heaven is portrayed as a kingdom: a realm where the lion lies down with the lamb and where no one hurts or destroys in God's holy mountain; a place where the hungry are fed, the homeless housed, and the sick healed; a place where death and suffering will be no more and God will wipe every tear from our eyes. Jesus speaks frequently of the kingdom of heaven, which is a synonym for the kingdom of God—a new creation where this fallen world is finally redeemed and transformed. In that sense heaven is a place. I will say more about this in later chapters.

But if Jesus is no more than our ticket to a wonderful place, if Jesus means nothing more to us than a means of getting to heaven, we are missing part of the point. John's gospel reminds us more powerfully than any other book of the Bible that heaven is a relationship with Jesus that can begin here and now.

I had an uncle who drove my grandparents crazy. He never went to church, and when my grandparents asked him about this, he said, "I'll make peace with God on my death bed." My father pointed out that he might not have the luxury of a death bed. He might die suddenly and not have the chance to make peace with God.

At the time I thought that was a good argument. Only later did I realize that both my uncle and my father were making the same assumption: that Jesus came to save us only after we die.

But what if Jesus came to save us before we die? John's gospel screams that message. "I am the way, the truth, and the life," Jesus says, not just in the future but now. "I am the resurrection and the life," Jesus says, not just in the future but now.

When Jesus says he goes to prepare a place for us, he is talking about his approaching death and resurrection. Jesus died and rose to prepare a place for us—a place with him, in a relationship to him that can transform our lives forever, beginning here and now.

The Successful Prodigal

One of Jesus' most famous parables is about a prodigal son. A father has two sons. The younger asks his father for his share of the inheritance. This would be scandalous in any culture, but especially so in a traditional Middle Eastern setting. In effect the son is saying to his father: "I am tired of waiting for you to die. My relationship to you means nothing, except for your money."

The father gives the younger son his share of the inheritance, and the son goes out and squanders it. When the money is gone, the son struggles to survive, ultimately finding work feeding some pigs (a humiliating thing for a Jewish person to do). Finally, when he hits bottom, the son realizes that his father's servants have it better than he does. So he goes back to his father, thinking he will ask to be taken back as a servant. Notice that the son is still thinking only of how he can benefit from his father's money. He does not expect to be treated like a son, but he is hoping at least for a place to live and food to eat.

The father, however, has been watching for him. He sees him coming from far off. The father does not wait for the son to arrive; he runs out to meet him. The son begins his well-rehearsed speech: "Father, I have sinned against heaven and before you; I am no longer worthy to be called your son" (Luke 15:21). But the father cuts him off and embraces him before the son gets to the part about being a servant.[14] Why? Because the father is not yearning for the son's labor but for a relationship with the son. The son is back! That is what the father cares about.

Later when the older son hears that his brother has come back and that their father has thrown a party for him, he is angry and refuses to come in. So the father goes out to him. Notice again how important to the father is his relationship with both sons. The father pleads with his older son to join the party. But the older son replies, "Listen! For all these years I have been working like a slave for you, and I have never disobeyed your command; yet you have never given me even a young goat so that I might celebrate with my friends" (Luke 15:29). Like the younger son, the older sees the father in terms of economic benefit. He fails to see that the greatest benefit is the relationship itself, being part of the father's family, something he has been blessed with all along.

This story raises an important question: Is faith worth it only when it gives us physical health, economic success, or personal status? Or is something more important involved? In a sense, the older brother is a successful prodigal. He is not dissolute or destitute, like the younger brother, but he too needs to return to the father. He is missing out on the party, which means missing out on the blessing of being part of the family.

The Christian faith cannot be reduced to ethics. The older son was obedient to the father's commands, but estranged. The father came out to find him, because the father is interested not only in obedience but in relationship. Things like worship, prayer, and listening to God's word in the scripture are important not only for making us better people but for expressing and nurturing our relationship to God, the relationship for which we were created.

Certainly, the Christian life includes service in God's name. Faith without works is dead. But so is works without faith. We were made for a relationship with God, and our hearts will be restless without one.

A Relationship Worth Having

As I mentioned earlier, I grew up in an Air Force family at a time when the Air Force moved families around about every year and a half. By the time I was in eighth grade I had lived in ten different houses and gone to seven different schools.

I remember feeling a little anxious each time we moved, wondering what our house would be like, what my school would be like, if my teacher would be nice, whether I would make friends. But I held on to the lesson that I had learned from my parents and Sunday School teachers: that God loved me and would be with me. I remember in Sunday School memorizing the verse from Joshua 1:9: "Be strong and courageous; do not be frightened or dismayed, for the Lord your God is with you wherever you go." I sometimes said that verse to myself when we moved to a new place and I started at a new school.

As a child it never occurred to me to wonder how my mother coped with all these moves. I knew that my mother was anxious about moving, just like I was, but she never seemed to be afraid. Even when my father was gone for long stretches of time and she was raising my brother and me by herself, she showed no fear.

I discovered why during her last year of life. I was visiting her in her assisted living facility, and out of the blue she said to me, "I love that song 'In the Garden.'" "In the Garden" is a song about Mary Magdalene meeting Jesus in the garden outside his tomb on Easter morning. Then my mother, without hesitation, began singing all the words of that song, including the chorus:

> And he walks with me and he talks with me,
> And he tells me I am his own;
> And the joy we share as we tarry there,
> None other has ever known.

At this point my mother's memory was rather shaky. She knew who I was, but sometimes she could not remember my name. So I said to her, "Mom, sometimes you can't even remember my name. How can you remember all the words of that song?" She said, "Sometimes when I sit here feeling sad and lonely, I remember this song, and I know I'm not alone."

That is the faith my mother passed on to me. Jesus is not just a memory but a presence in our lives. He walks with us and talks with us and tells us we are his own. I cannot prove that happens. I can only say that I have experienced it, and it is a faith worth believing.

Questions for Discussion

1. Describe a person who has shaped your understanding or experience of God for good or for bad. How did that affect your beliefs?
2. Where in your life do you learn things about God that you do not already know or think? Where do you encounter opportunities for your picture of God to be challenged?
3. What is prayer like for you? What do you say when you pray? What do you experience?
4. When has God felt most personal to you? When has God felt distant or absent? How have your beliefs about God shaped those experiences?

2

What's Wrong with Us?

At the heart of the Christian faith is the belief that God sent Jesus to save us. But from what exactly do we need saving?

I was not what you would call a troubled child, or even a troubled teenager. I did what my parents said, mostly. I got good grades in school, avoided fights, drugs, and criminal behavior, generally came home when I was supposed to, got only one traffic ticket (driving without my headlights on), and was an Eagle Scout, not to mention going to church and participating in the youth group. I was generally regarded as a good kid. So why did I need "saving"?

The first answer was a nagging thought that despite being a good kid I was not good enough for God. I remember being particularly unnerved when I heard the parable that Jesus tells in Matthew 25 of the last judgment. The Son of Man—meaning Jesus—sits on his throne, separating people as a shepherd separates the sheep from the goats. To those on his right Jesus says,

> Come, you that are blessed by my Father, inherit the kingdom prepared for you from the foundation of the world; for I was hungry and you gave me food, I was thirsty and you gave me something to drink, I was a stranger and you welcomed me, I was naked and you gave me clothing, I was sick and you took care of me, I was in prison and you visited me (Matthew 25:34-36).

They reply in effect, "What are you talking about? We never did any of these things for you." But Jesus answers, "Truly I tell you, just as you did it to one of the least of these who are members of my family, you did it to me" (Matthew 25:40).

Then Jesus addresses those on his left:

> You that are accursed, depart from me into the eternal fire prepared for the devil and his angels; for I was hungry and you gave me no food, I was thirsty and you gave me nothing to drink, I was a stranger and you did not welcome me, naked and you did not give me clothing, sick and in prison and you did not visit me (Matthew 25:41-43).

Those on the left protest: "Lord, when was it that we saw you hungry or thirsty or a stranger or naked or sick or in prison, and did not take care of you?" (Matthew 25:44). Then Jesus answers, "Truly I tell you, just as you did not do it to one of the least of these, you did not do it to me" (Matthew 25:45).

To a conscientious boy who cared about being accepted by God, this was a scary parable. It told me that staying out of trouble is not enough. God is interested in what we do for others, especially people in need.

One day, as an 11-year-old, I passed an elderly blind man sitting on a street corner with a sign asking for money. I walked hurriedly past, but later thought, "There is a person in need that I did not help." And I thought of Jesus saying, "As you did not do it to one of the least of these, you did not do it to me." So the next time I went into town with my parents, I took a dollar bill, and when I saw him on the street I went over and put the dollar bill in his hat. That made me feel better for a while, but then I encountered the next panhandler and the next Salvation Army bell ringer, not to mention the pictures on television of refugees and starving children all over the world. I felt overwhelmed and guilty.

In the next chapter I will say more about what helped me deal with this guilt. In many ways my feelings of guilt were misplaced. I was putting too much responsibility on my 11-year-old shoulders. But later in my life, reflecting on Jesus' parable and my encounter with the panhandler, I gained new insights into why we need saving.

It's Not Just About Me

When I was in high school, a new youth pastor came to our church. He led Bible studies on passages like Amos 5:21-24, where the Lord says through the prophet Amos:

> I hate, I despise your festivals, and I take no delight in your solemn assemblies. Even though you offer me your burnt offerings and grain offerings, I will not accept them; … But let justice roll down like waters, and righteousness like an everflowing stream.

My friends and I in the youth group had never heard this scripture before. Then he read to us verses from the gospel of Luke, verses I had heard before but to which I had not really paid attention, such as the song of Mary in Luke 1:

> [God] has shown strength with his arm; he has scattered the proud in the thoughts of their hearts. He has brought down the powerful from their thrones, and lifted up the lowly; he has filled the hungry with good things, and sent the rich away empty (Luke 1:51-53).

In 1971, with growing protests against the Vietnam War and rising racial tensions in blighted cities, these verses awakened new issues in my religious conscience. Suddenly following Jesus was not just a matter of personal morality but concern for the world: concern about peace, the environment, justice for the lowly, and empowerment for racially and economically disadvantaged people. As we discussed these issues on my high school debate team, I gained appreciation for their complexity, but at church I gained new appreciation for how God cares about these issues and wants us to care about them. I realized that Jesus came not just to save us from our individual guilt but to save a fallen world, including blind people panhandling on street corners and refugees around the world who are homeless and starving. Jesus came not just so I could be put right with God but so that the whole world could be put right with God.

Where do we get the idea of "right"?

Before I discuss this further, I must digress into a philosophical question. I first encountered this question in college from the same philosophy professor who introduced me to Nietzsche. From where do we get the ideas of "right" and "good"?

One need not believe in God to sense there is something wrong with the world. Acknowledging evil was the premise for my high school friend Mike's argument against God. But the very notion of evil introduces into the conversation categories of right and wrong, good and bad. From where do these ideas come?

C. S. Lewis begins his defense of Christianity precisely at this point. In the opening chapter of *Mere Christianity* he writes,

> Every one has heard people quarreling. ... They say things like this: "How'd you like it if anyone did the same to you?"—"That's my seat, I was there first"—"Leave him alone, he isn't doing any harm" ... "Come on, you promised."

> Now what interests me about all these remarks is that the man who makes them is not merely saying that the other man's behavior does not happen to please him. He is appealing to some kind of standard of behavior which he expects the other man to know about. And the other man very seldom replies, "To hell with your standard." Nearly always he tries to make out that what he has done does not really go against the standard, or that if it does there is some special excuse.[1]

The very existence of such a conversation, Lewis points out, suggests a view of right and wrong that exists beyond our individual preference.

My friend Mike shared this assumption when he asked me, "Do you also admit that there is evil in the world?" The question implies a concept of evil that Mike assumes I will share. There is in both of our minds a common standard telling us that the world isn't "right."

But where do we get these notions of right and wrong, good and evil? Science can tell us how things are, and how things might be related. For example, science can investigate a possible link between carbon emissions and climate change, then forecast the effects of climate change on coastal cities. But science cannot tell us whether those effects will be good or bad, because the question of how the world "ought" to be is not an empirical question. It is a question related to the values of the people discussing it.

Values are personal. They derive from beings who have choice, purpose, and intention. I am content to leave some values to individual preference. Blue may be my favorite color, but if you prefer green, that is your business. I am unlikely to say you *should* like one or the other. But when it comes to values like truthfulness, fairness, justice, or helping the helpless—we tend to think of these not as preferences but as things that should be considered good by everyone. Admittedly there may be situations that require a nuanced application of these values. We might make an allowance for someone who hedges truthfulness to spare someone's feelings, or who treats two children differently because they have different needs. But these examples illustrate Lewis' point. When not strictly following one of these values, we tend to feel that an explanation is required. We feel a need to justify our actions, which would be unnecessary if we did not regard certain values as applying to all of us.

But here is the dilemma. Values are rooted in persons, not things. Yet we regard certain values as transcending personal preference. From where do they get this standing? We might argue that certain values make sense because they make life better for more people, but even then we introduce a concept of "better" with which we assume others will agree—with which we think they should agree.

If values come from the persons who do the valuing, and yet we believe that certain values, like truthfulness, justice, or compassion, should apply to all people, that their validity transcends personal preference, then their source must lie in a *Person who transcends persons*. The very idea of "should" suggests someone with a capacity for choice, purpose, and intention, someone who has the authority to give certain values a prescriptive meaning for all of us. The idea of "should," when pressed hard enough, ultimately requires a personal God.

We see this argument in the Declaration of Independence: "We hold these truths to be self-evident, that all men are created equal, that they are endowed by their Creator with certain unalienable Rights, that among these are Life, Liberty, and the pursuit of Happiness." Even while appealing to self-evident truths—principles presumed to be innate or instinctual for human beings—the framers of the Declaration also appealed to an authority higher than themselves and, more importantly, higher than the British king. To make their argument in the world of public opinion, they appealed to principles of how the world ought to be, regardless of the self-interested views of the colonists or the British monarch.

Near the end of Dostoyevsky's novel *The Brothers Karamazov*, Dmitri Karamazov is imprisoned for murdering his father. He tells his brother Alyosha that he is not worried about the upcoming trial. He says,

> It's God that's worrying me. That's the only thing that's worrying me. What if He doesn't exist? What if Rakitin's right—that it's an idea made up by men? Then, if He doesn't exist, man is the king of the earth, of the universe. Magnificent! Only how is he going to be good without God? That's the question. I always come back to that. Who is man going to love then? To whom will he be thankful? ... Rakitin says that one can love humanity instead of God. ... [He says] "You'd better think about the extension of

civic rights, or of keeping down the price of meat. You will show your love for humanity more simply and directly by that, than by philosophy." I answered him, "Well, but you, without God, are more likely to raise the price of meat, if it suits you, and make a rouble on every penny."

Dmitri concludes that without God, "everything is lawful."[2]

Of course people who do not believe in God can still act in loving ways if they choose. But there is no standard to say they should act in loving ways. If all right and wrong is ultimately a matter of human decision, right is determined by those who have the power to enforce their will on others. A reasoned appeal to transcendent values gives way to impassioned rhetoric appealing to the self-interest of enough voters to get elected. Might—whether in the form of ballots or guns—makes right.

In an article called "Guilt, Victimhood, and Moral Indignation," David Brooks writes,

We still use words describing virtue and vice, but without any overall metaphysics. Religious frameworks no longer organize public debate. Secular philosophies that grew out of the enlightenment have fallen apart. We have words and emotional instincts about what feels right and wrong, but no settled criteria to help us think, argue, and decide.[3]

In the science fiction show *Humans*, robotics engineers armed with powerful computer programs have created synthetic humans, called synths, who develop consciousness, feelings, and aspirations. One named Hester becomes a sort of robotic supremacist who begins to despise her human programmers. At one point she says to a human, "Human lives have no inherent value. It just felt that way to you because there was no competing intelligence to offer an alternative view."[4]

Two observations about this statement: 1) it links values to a valuing agent—an intelligent being with the capacity to assign value to something, and 2) it suggests that competing valuing agents effectively neutralize any claims to inherent value. In other words, humans have no inherent value unless there is someone above humans, robots, or any other created being that gives them their value.

The Christian faith declares that humans have value, not because we say so, but because God says so. Our inherent value comes from a source above humans or any other being in this universe. It comes from the God who created it.

The Good World that God Intends

At this point I began to read the Bible with new eyes, looking for what God considers good. I noticed that six times in the opening chapter of Genesis, God looks at the newly created world and says, "It is good." This is not a scientific statement. It is a values statement, a religious statement.

In Genesis 2 we get a more detailed picture of this good world:

> And the Lord God planted a garden in Eden, in the east; and there he put the man whom he had formed. Out of the ground the Lord God made to grow every tree that is pleasant to the sight and good for food, the tree of life also in the midst of the garden, and the tree of the knowledge of good and evil (Genesis 2:8-9).

Later in the chapter we are told about the creation of animals and the harmonious relationship they have with the human being who gives them names. Then we have the creation of another person, and they find joy and support in their relationship.

Like Genesis 1, Genesis 2 deals in images and metaphor. But notice the kind of reality portrayed by these images. God has created a world with plenty of food. And not just food, but beauty and truth and loving relationships—all the things that make life worth living. That is how the world is supposed to be. The world was not created to be a place where nature must be despoiled in order for people to have what they need. Nor is it a place where some must go without the necessities of life in order for others to have more. But something has gone wrong. Things aren't the way they are supposed to be.

What Went Wrong?

How could it be that God created the world good, but now it is not good? Or to echo the question of my friend Mike: how could a loving and all-powerful God allow evil into the world?

In Genesis 3 a serpent strikes up a conversation with the first woman. At this point we are not meant to ask who the serpent is or why the serpent can talk. We are meant to pay attention to the conversation. The serpent says, "Did God say, 'You shall not eat of the fruit of the trees in the garden?'" (Genesis 3:1). We know this is not true, and so does the woman. God created a good world with plenty of food for human beings and animals. But the serpent plants in the woman a seed of doubt, causing her to wonder if she could have more.

The woman says to the serpent, "We may eat the fruit of the trees in the garden; but God said, 'You shall not eat of the fruit of the tree that is in the middle of the garden, nor shall you touch it, or you shall die'" (Genesis 3:2-3). This is the tree of the knowledge of good and evil mentioned in Genesis 2. But the serpent says to the woman, "You will not die; for God knows that when you eat of it your eyes will be opened, and you will be like God, knowing good and evil" (Genesis 3:4-5).

In this case "knowing good and evil" does not mean being educated about right and wrong. The woman and man already know about right and wrong. They already know God's command regarding the forbidden fruit. In this case "knowing good and evil" means having the power to decide for themselves what is good and evil, right and wrong. In other words, to be their own gods.[5]

This temptation has been repeated throughout history: from every dictator who hoped to rule the world, to every lowly person who wanted to be the captain of his or her own soul. In the book *Habits of the Heart*, sociologist Robert Bellah interviews a young nurse named Sheila Larson. She tells him, "I can't remember the last time I went to church, [but] my faith has carried me a long way. It's Sheilaism. Just my own little voice."[6]

That is the original temptation: to be our own gods, to have our own self-contained religion, to know good and evil in the sense of deciding it for ourselves.

When the first man and woman gave into this temptation, there followed a cascade of effects. Genesis 3:7 says, "Then the eyes of both were opened, and they knew they were naked; and they sewed fig leaves together and made loincloths for themselves." This surely does not mean that Adam and Eve were oblivious to their nakedness before eating the forbidden fruit. Rather it means that now, for the first time, they are *ashamed*. In one of the many ironies of this story, they set out to become gods and end up ashamed of being human.

People are the most inhuman when trying to be God. Consider all of the world's dictators. Those with the greatest desire for control had the greatest capacity for evil. Nor is this limited to dictators. Parents who desire the most control over their children can be the cruelest, and husbands or wives who want the most power over their spouses are the most abusive. When we try to become God, we become less than human.

But there is more. The next verse says, "They heard the sound of the Lord God walking in the garden at the time of the evening breeze, and the man and his wife hid themselves from the presence of the Lord among the trees of the garden." As we saw in chapter 1, we were created for a relationship with God. But when we try to become our own gods, we lose the best thing about being human, the very thing that gives us dignity.

From these two calamities come other ripple effects. In Genesis 3:16 God says to the woman, "I will greatly increase your pangs in childbearing; in pain you shall bring forth children, yet your desire shall be for your husband, and he shall rule over you." Note that the idea of husbands ruling over their wives is not the way it was supposed to be. It is a ripple effect of our broken relationship with God. So is the pain associated with bearing and raising children. Family trauma is not how the world was meant to be.

Then in Genesis 3:17-18 God says to the man,

> Because you have listened to the voice of your wife and have eaten of the tree about which I commanded you, 'You shall not eat of it,' cursed is the ground because of you; in toil you shall eat of it all the days of your life; thorns and thistles it shall bring forth for you; and you shall eat the plants of the field.

Again note the symbolism of the description. The Bible is not saying that work is a punishment for sin. God created people to till the garden and keep it (Genesis 2:15). But work was meant to be productive and fulfilling. Frustrating, meaningless, and unproductive work is not what God intended for us.

Finally we are told at the end of Genesis 3 that God drives the man and woman out of the garden of Eden and sets a guard so that they cannot eat of the tree of life (Genesis 3:24). The tree of life is not the same as the tree of the knowledge of good and evil which God had commanded them not to eat. The tree of life was not originally withheld from the humans. Presumably they might have eaten of that tree and lived forever. But now as a result of trying to be their own gods, that tree is taken away, and soon death will enter the world.

A Broken Relationship with God and a Broken Creation

It is amazing how fast things deteriorate after the first temptation. In Genesis 4 we have the first murder: Cain killing his brother Abel. Two chapters later in Genesis 6 we read:

> The Lord saw that the wickedness of humankind was great in the earth, and that every inclination of

the thoughts of their hearts was only evil continually. And the Lord was sorry that he had made humankind on the earth, and it grieved him to his heart. So the Lord said, "I will blot out from the earth the human beings I have created—people together with animals and creeping things and birds of the air, for I am sorry that I made them." But Noah found favor in the sight of the Lord (Genesis 6:5-8).

In a Public Television series called *Genesis: A Living Conversation*, Bill Moyers hosted a panel of people from different religious, ethnic, and professional backgrounds discussing the story of Noah and the flood.[7] Barney, an editor for the *Wall Street Journal* said,

> I first heard this story as a child in Sunday School, and then it was all about rainbows and the fun of getting on the Ark and going for a sail with all those animals. It was like your own personal zoo. Coming back to this story as an adult, I'm struck by the awfulness of God destroying the whole earth.[8]

Karen, a former Roman Catholic nun, said,

> I didn't think about the coziness of the Ark when I was a child. I was thinking about a frightening God. So that when you're later told that "God so loved the world that he sent his only begotten son," you think, "Yes, but what about Noah? What about the flood?"[9]

I confess that as a child I too was frightened by the idea of God flooding the world.

For some this story suggests a God not worth believing in, a God who would engage in mass extermination instead of rehabilitation. My friend Mike would have lifted it up as Exhibit A for a God who is all-powerful but not very loving.

But over the years as I have studied this story, I have gained a new perspective on it. What if the holocaust was already happening at the beginning of the story before God intervened? What if the evil mentioned in Genesis 6:5 was on the order of Hitler's genocide? How much suffering and destruction did the nation of Germany experience, not to mention the world, before Hitler was finally stopped? And how many men, women, children, and even animals lost their lives in the process?

Or consider the evil of slavery in America. How much suffering, destruction, and death had to take place in this country before slavery was finally ended? I think of Abraham Lincoln's words during his Second Inaugural Address four years into the Civil War:

> Fondly do we hope—fervently do we pray—that this mighty scourge of war may speedily pass away. Yet, if God wills that it continue, until all the wealth piled by the bond-men's two hundred and fifty years of unrequited toil shall be sunk, and until every drop of blood drawn with the lash, shall be paid by another drawn by the sword, as was said three thousand years ago, so still it must be said "the judgments of the Lord, are true and righteous altogether."

Real evil is not overcome by a smile and a wave of the hand, even by God. Serious evil always produces unspeakable suffering before it is stopped, and the flood in the time of Noah is a horrifying portrayal of that truth.

Another example is the story of the Exodus. Pharaoh's oppression of the Hebrew slaves was a precursor of the Holocaust. To keep the Hebrew slaves from becoming too numerous and threatening their Egyptian masters, Pharaoh orders all the Hebrew male babies to be drowned in the Nile River. But God determines to save them through a series of plagues brought upon the Egyptians to force Pharaoh to set the Hebrews free.

In one sense the plagues are God's judgment on the Egyptians for their oppression, just as the flood was God's judgment on a world of evil. But in another sense, the plagues are the outworking of that evil—its ripple effect. Recall that the Egyptians were killing Hebrew babies in the Nile River.

So what is the first plague? The Nile turns to blood. Then frogs are driven out of the river and infest the land: the second plague. The frogs die and the land swarms with gnats and flies: the third and fourth plagues. The gnats and flies spread disease among the cattle: fifth plague. Eventually, the disease kills the Egyptian first born male children at the time of the Passover. The ripple effect of sin comes full circle.

At the end of the first Gulf war as Iraqi troops fled Kuwait, they set fire to oil wells all over the country. Skies were blackened, birds disappeared, burning oil seared what little vegetation was left, leaving camels to search in vain for food. It was not only people who suffered as a result of that war but the whole creation.

The New Testament hints at this in Romans 8:

> We know that the whole creation has been groaning in labor pains until now; and not only the creation but we ourselves, who have the first fruits of the Spirit, groan inwardly while we wait for adoption, the redemption of our bodies (Romans 8:22-23).

The story of Noah illustrates a recurring truth: that the destructiveness of human evil ripples out to engulf innocent people and will eventually destroy the whole creation, unless God intervenes. But this is not done easily, nor without cost. More about this in chapter 4.

The "Nature" of Christian Hope

In *The Dialogues of Plato*, Socrates argues that the best hope for human beings is to be rid of their bodies. He says,

> For the body is a source of endless trouble by reason of the mere requirement of food; and is liable also to diseases which overtake and impede us in the search after true being: it fills us full of loves, and lusts, and fears, and fancies of all kinds, and endless foolery. ... Whence comes wars and fightings and factions? Whence but from the body and the lusts of the body? ... It has been proved to us by experience

> that if we would have pure knowledge of anything
> we must be quit of the body—the soul in herself
> must behold things in themselves; ... not while we
> live, but after death. ... And thus having got rid of
> the foolishness of the body we shall be pure and hold
> converse with the pure, and know of ourselves the
> clear light everywhere, which is no other than the
> light of truth.[10]

There is an interesting similarity between this view of
life after death and those who come back from near death
experiences and report the sensation of leaving their bodies
behind and entering a tunnel of light into a realm untroubled
by things earthly or tangible.

But this is not the story of Jesus' resurrection. Jesus did
not ascend to heaven and leave his body behind. The tomb
was empty. All four gospels make that point. Jesus rose from
the dead, body and all. He shows the disciples his hands and
feet to prove that he is not a ghost or a spirit. In Luke's gospel
he even eats some fish to show that he has a real body.

But it is a transformed body. It will never die again. It is
no longer subject to decay. And it can show up among the
disciples even behind locked doors. Jesus' resurrection was
not an example of his soul leaving bodily life behind. It was
an example of God transforming bodily life to make it what
it was meant to be all along.

God's goal is not to pull us out of this world, leaving
behind a creation still racked by violence, injustice, and
suffering. God's goal is the redemption of creation. The last
book of the Bible, the book of Revelation, pictures God's
reign over a new heaven and earth (Revelation 21:1), a place
where the tree of life from the Garden of Eden will be brought
back providing year-round fruit and leaves "for the healing
of the nations" (Revelation 22:2).

My friend Mike might ask why God did not prevent evil
from happening in the first place. But if people are created
for a relationship with God, they must have the freedom to
choose that relationship or not. In a sense Mike is right when
he says that God is not all-powerful. In creating human

beings God accepts a limitation on God's power. God will not control human beings like puppets. But that does not mean God is helpless in the face of evil.

The Christian faith confronts the reality of evil and suffering with three truths:

1. God created the world to be good, including the fact that human beings are given free will to do good or evil.
2. Because humans choose evil, the world is not the way it is supposed to be.
3. God has not given up on the creation or its human inhabitants. There is hope, but it is not an easy hope nor without suffering.

After the flood, God has a change of heart, like the change of heart we saw in Hosea 11. Noah builds an altar to the Lord and offers on it a burnt offering in gratitude for God rescuing them. Genesis 8:21 says,

> And when the Lord smelled the pleasing odor, the Lord said in his heart, "I will never again curse the ground because of humankind, for the inclination of the human heart is evil from youth; nor will I ever again destroy every living creature."

"The inclination of the human heart is evil." Note that God said this before the flood (Genesis 6:5), and now God admits that it is still true after the flood. But this time God vows never again to destroy every living creature. So what is God going to do? That is the subject of chapter 4. But first we must look at the fixes that have not worked.

Questions for Discussion

1. Where do you find your own moral compass? What guides your thoughts about whether a particular action is right or wrong?
2. In the areas of politics, work, or daily life, how do you discuss the rightness or wrongness of a particular action? To what reasons do you appeal?

3. How would you explain to a child (or an adult) why there are earthquakes that wipe out entire communities or terrorist bombings that destroy innocent lives? How do you describe God's relationship to these things?

4. What would you most like to change about our world? What gives you hope that it could happen?

3

Fixes That Have Not Worked

I have preached many sermons and taught many Bible studies on the story of Noah, but I witnessed a new approach in the 2014 film *Noah* directed by Darren Aronofsky. In Aronofsky's film, Noah comes to the conclusion that God does not intend to save humanity by means of the ark. The ark is mainly for the animals. Humans are invited along only to take care of the animals while on the boat. Once the flood has receded and the animals are released, Noah believes that humans are supposed to die off, so that animals and the rest of creation can live in peace.

It is an intriguing thought. If the destruction of God's good creation is the ripple effect of human wrongdoing, then how can God save humans without imperiling the creation? But if humans are allowed to become extinct, what happens to God's relationship with them, the relationship for which they were made in God's image? Is there any option by which God can save both creation and humanity?

Some Approaches to the Problem

In William Golding's book *Lord of the Flies*, a group of British boys are stranded on a deserted Pacific island during World War II, the only survivors of a plane crash that killed all the adults on board. The boys are young, ranging in age from about 5 to 12. Fortunately, the island provides for all their physical needs: plenty of food and water, as well as temperatures warm enough not to need shelter or extra clothes.

The situation provides a test for this question: What would happen if a group of children had the chance to build a new society, like Noah and his family?

At first, things go reasonably well. The children elect a leader, adopt some rules, and cooperate on several important tasks. But soon things begin to unravel. It starts with name-calling. Then there are minor skirmishes. Some of the boys neglect their job tending the signal fire, and a ship passes without seeing the smoke. This leads to recriminations and finally a split in the group. One of the boys takes part of the group to another side of the island. The two groups start fighting, and near the end two children are killed and a large part of the island goes up in flames.

The children are finally rescued by a British naval cruiser. But even this has a certain irony. While the children are fighting each other on the island, the adults are fighting each other across the globe. A naval officer stops the children from destroying each other. But who will save the adults from the same fate?

Near the beginning of their time on the island, the boys adopt rules. One approach to the problem of human wrongdoing is legislation—passing laws that will curb human greed and self-centeredness. The boys adopt rules to make their island safe and enhance their chances of rescue. But the rules are broken.

The same happens with adults. The U.S. Criminal Code has about 23,000 pages. Many of these laws were added because people kept finding new ways to hurt or take advantage of each other. The U.S. Tax Code has over 74,000 pages, which is about triple the number it had in 1980. Many of these pages were added to prevent people from taking unfair advantage of earlier regulations.

Laws have never been successful at making people good. In the book of Romans the apostle Paul writes, "For I delight in the law of God in my inmost self, but I see in my members another law at war with the law of my mind, making me a captive to the law of sin that dwells in my members" (Romans 7:22-23). Rules, laws, and codes of conduct do not solve the problem.

Another approach is education. If people were properly instructed, could the world become the good place it was meant to be? Moses tells the people of Israel, "Keep these words that I am commanding you today in your heart. Recite them to your children and talk about them when you are at home and when you are away, when you lie down and when you rise" (Deuteronomy 6:6-7). Do this, he says, "so that it may go well with you, and so that you may multiply greatly in a land flowing with milk and honey, as the Lord, the God of your ancestors, has promised you" (Deuteronomy 6:3).

The book of Proverbs is filled with attempts to impart righteousness by education. "Hear, my child, and accept my words, that the years of your life may be many. ... Keep hold of instruction; do not let her go; guard her, for she is your life" (Proverbs 4:10, 13). Later the prophets are sent to the people of Israel to teach them, and in many cases to confront them:

- "Learn to do good; seek justice, rescue the oppressed, defend the orphan, plead for the widow" (Isaiah 1:17).
- "But let justice roll down like waters, and righteousness like an everflowing stream" (Amos 5:24).
- "He has told you, O mortal, what is good; and what does the Lord require of you but to do justice, and to love kindness, and to walk humbly with your God" (Micah 6:8).

The Bible records countless attempts to educate people on the right way to live, but it does no good. God says to the prophet Ezekiel: "But the house of Israel will not listen to you for they are not willing to listen to me; because all the house of Israel have a hard forehead and a stubborn heart" (Ezekiel 3:7). Despite having God's commandments and numerous educators to guide them, the people of Israel turn their backs on God and are driven out of the Promised Land, just as Adam and Eve were driven out of the Garden of Eden.

Attacking Evil with New Leadership

Often people approach the world's problems by seeking new political leadership. Some of the boys on the island split off from the others and choose a new leader, hoping that the new leader will make things better.

The Israelites tried this in the time of the judges. The book of Judges describes a revolving door of leaders for the people of Israel. Some were better than others, but none were able to make the nation of Israel into the blessing they were meant to be. So in the next book of the Bible—I Samuel—the people ask for a king. They think that having a powerful monarch will finally give them security.

One wonders how many dictators have arisen because people thought a strong central leader would give them security and prosperity.

But it did not work. Samuel gives this dramatic warning about the dangers of a king:

> These will be the ways of the king who will reign over you: he will take your sons and appoint them to his chariots and to be his horsemen, and to run before his chariots; and he will appoint for himself commanders of thousands and commanders of fifties, and some to plow his ground and to reap his harvest, and to make his implements of war and the equipment of his chariots. He will take your daughters to be perfumers and cooks and bakers. He will take the best of your fields and vineyards and olive orchards and give them to his courtiers. He will take one-tenth of your grain and of your vineyards and give it to his officers and his courtiers. He will take your male and female slaves, and the best of your cattle and donkeys, and put them to his work. He will take one-tenth of your flocks, and you shall be his slaves. And in that day you will cry out because of your king, whom you have chosen for yourselves; but the LORD will not answer you in that day (I Samuel 8:11-18).

Kings are infected with the same problems as the rest of us. But because they are more powerful, their self-centeredness is more destructive. The crucifixion of Jesus exposes the lie that the kingdom of God could come through Caesar. The Holocaust does the same in the case of Hitler, as does the Gulag in the case of Lenin. In each of these situations people gave their allegiance to a political power believing that it would give them security and blessing. What they got instead was injustice and suffering on a horrifying scale.

Lesslie Newbigin writes,

> Certainly, a church that sees the cross of Jesus as the central event of history can never identify any political order with the reign of God. ... It is only possible to entertain that idea if one denies the biblical account of the radical sinfulness of human nature, a sinfulness that no social order will remove.[1]

The Root of the Problem

In one of my college classes I was introduced to the writings of Aleksandr Solzhenitsyn. Solzhenitsyn spent years as a political prisoner in the Gulag—the Soviet Union's prison system. During his imprisonment he witnessed many acts of good and evil, sometimes committed by the same person. He writes,

> If only there were evil people somewhere insidiously committing evil deeds, and it were necessary only to separate them from the rest of us and destroy them. But the line dividing good and evil cuts through the heart of every human being. And who is willing to destroy a piece of his own heart?[2]

In the last chapter I talked about being a good kid and wondering why I needed saving. Then in high school, thanks to a youth pastor with a social conscience, I realized that Jesus came not just to save me but to save the world, to bring God's righteousness and peace to a world of violence, injustice, and suffering.

But reading Solzhenitsyn's words gave voice to something that I finally had to admit to myself: that I, too, shared in the problem; that pride, jealousy, anger, lust, and greed could also be found in my own heart and in my own reaction to situations; that even if I was not violent, I could certainly be unkind, and even if I did not yearn for power, I certainly yearned for status and was jealous of those who had more of it than I did.

Early in the book of Romans, Paul condemns the idolatry of Gentiles, but then he turns to his own people, the Jews. He says, "Are we any better off? No, not at all; for we have already charged that all, both Jews and Greeks, are under the power of sin" (Romans 3:9). Then alluding to Psalm 14, he says, "There is no one who is righteous, not even one; there is no one who has understanding, there is no one who seeks God. All have turned aside, together they have become worthless; there is no one who shows kindness, there is not even one" (Romans 3:10-11).

Admittedly this all sounds rather negative, like a faith *not* worth believing. But when rightly understood, the realization that all of us are sinners can give us humility, compassion, and hope. In his book *People of the Lie*, Scott Peck writes,

> Evil is not committed by people who feel uncertain about their righteousness, who question their own motives, who worry about betraying themselves. The evil in this world is committed by the spiritual fat cats, by the Pharisees of our own day, the self-righteous who think they are without sin. ... Unpleasant though it may be, the sense of personal sin is precisely that which keeps our sin from getting out of hand. It is quite painful at times, but it is a very great blessing because it is our one and only effective safeguard against our own proclivity for evil.[3]

The first step in Alcoholics Anonymous says, "We admitted that we were powerless over alcohol—that our lives had become unmanageable." The first step in recovery from addiction is realizing that we cannot solve this problem by ourselves.

The same is true for the problem which the Bible calls sin. Sin is more than a particular thought or action which violates God's commandments. It is less like an infraction, and more like an infection or an addiction. It is a condition that holds us in its grip. Like an alcoholic we may mask this condition behind the façade of a well-functioning life, but left untreated it will destroy us.

Most of us are less like the prodigal son and more like the older brother. We are not dissolute bums surviving off the swill we steal from the pigs. We are dutiful children working hard in the family business. But resentment is just under the surface. As is jealousy, pride, greed, and other things that keep us from the joy and community that God meant for us.

Jesus tells a parable about a Pharisee who enters the temple, stands by himself away from others, and prays, "God, I thank you that I am not like other people: thieves, rogues, adulterers, or even like this tax collector" (Luke 18:11). He could have added alcoholics, drug addicts, corrupt politicians, or greedy CEOs. He was good at identifying the sins of others but oblivious to the sin in himself.

C. S. Lewis once wrote an essay called "The Trouble with 'X'", where 'X' stands for anyone who creates problems in your life. Interestingly, he wrote this essay for a church newsletter, which meant he had church people in mind. He writes,

[God] sees (like you) how all the people in your home or your job are in various degrees awkward or difficult; but when He looks into that home or factory or office He sees one more person of the same kind—the one you never do see. I mean, of course, yourself. … You also have a fatal flaw in your character. All the hopes and plans of others have again and again shipwrecked on your character just as your hopes and plans have shipwrecked on theirs. … And it is almost certainly something you don't know about—like what the advertisements call 'halitosis,' which everyone notices except the person who has it.[4]

That is the story of the Pharisee in Luke 18. By external measures he seems like a good person. He gives ten percent of his income to the church. What pastor would criticize that? His problem is not his generosity but his blindness to his own situation. His sense of superiority alienates him from everyone—not just the tax collector, but everyone. Even when he goes to the temple, he prays by himself, not wanting to associate with other people. And in the process he alienates himself from God.

Of course, we can also have the opposite problem: having too low an opinion about ourselves, thinking that we are hopelessly unworthy of a relationship with God or anyone else. But when we realize that sin is a condition of our humanness, and not just a failure of personal discipline or self-improvement, then we can be a little less harsh on ourselves and a little more open to God's grace.

The Antidote of Grace

My high school debate partner Mike grew up Roman Catholic, which in his case meant feeling a lot of guilt. Weekly confession left him with a sense that he would never be good enough to be accepted by God or make it to heaven.

I had some of the same feelings growing up in Protestant churches. At times I heard sermons every bit as guilt-producing as anything Mike heard in the Roman Catholic Church. I remember as an 11-year-old feeling afraid of God, fearing that I would never be good enough to be accepted in heaven.

Mike and I talked about this one time. We discovered that we dealt with our fear of God in opposite ways. Mike dealt with it by rejecting God. He decided there was no God out there to punish people or send them to hell. When we die, that is it. So the best we can do is enjoy ourselves each day in whatever way we can. His was the philosophy of Zarathustra.

The problem was that Mike never really did enjoy himself, because he found no meaning for his life. He got a PhD in economics and taught at several universities, but his life, as he himself put it, seemed empty.

I could have ended up like Mike. Even though he was Catholic and I was Protestant, I too grew up being afraid of God and fearful I might end up in hell. But fortunately there were pastors, Sunday School teachers, and Vacation Bible School leaders who told me over and over about God's grace.

I was especially helped by reading a biography of Martin Luther. I discovered that as a young man Luther was afraid of God, just as I was. He did religious works of all kinds to make up for this, just like the Pharisee in Jesus' parable. He went to church all the time. He prayed and read the Bible. He even entered a monastery where he thought he would be safe from temptation to sin. Except for the monastery, I did many of the same things.

But while he was reading the Bible, Martin Luther came across Romans 3, where the apostle Paul says, "Since all have sinned and fall short of the glory of God; they are now justified by his grace as a gift through the redemption that is in Christ Jesus" (Romans 3:23-24).

Those verses were a life-changing gift to Martin Luther, and when I read them, they became a life-changing gift to me. Instead of rejecting God in order to feel safe, I could embrace God and know that God's love for me is greater than my ability to mess it up.

So it was for the tax collector in Jesus' parable. He knew he was unworthy. He knew that by his own good works he would never earn God's favor. But instead of fleeing from God, he flung himself on God's mercy. He prayed, "God, be merciful to me a sinner" (Luke 18:13).

Jesus says that the tax collector went home *justified*, using the same word that Paul uses in Romans 3. The word justified means "put right." When we try to justify ourselves to God, as the Pharisee did, it does not work. But when we give up trying to justify ourselves, we are put right with God by grace. We are given a new relationship with God based not on our goodness but on God's transforming power. We do not come to God at the end of a long process of self-improvement; we come to God as addicts willing to be transformed by love.

Recognizing our sinfulness has three personal implications:

1. It takes away the pride that can make us insufferably arrogant.
2. It gives us empathy and openness toward others.
3. It allows us to be more open to God.

When we accept God's grace instead of thinking we don't need it, we become a little less judgmental and a little more compassionate; we become a little less driven to prove ourselves and a little more grateful for the experience of undeserved love.

G. K. Chesterton once observed that original sin "is the only part of Christian theology that can really be proved."[5]

I cannot prove that God exists, but by almost any definition of "good" the world does not measure up. The world is not the way it is supposed to be, and centuries of legislation, education, and attempts at political reform have not solved the problem. What will?

Questions for Discussion

1. What are some of the problems you see in our world that have not been solved by education, legislation, or political reform?
2. What issues in your life or world might be better handled if people were more humble—if they were less sure of their own "rightness"?
3. Are there any people in your life who provide you with honest feedback—helping you see issues in your own life to which you may have been blind? Who are they? How do they do this?
4. Have you ever felt anxious that you are not "good enough"? What made you feel that way? What helped you deal with that feeling?

4

Divine Intervention

In the last two chapters I talked about my growing realization that we need saving; not just me, but the whole world. And the things we have tried up to this point have not worked. But how is Jesus different? Why can Jesus save us when education, legislation, and therapy cannot?

Saved from the Outside-In

To explain this let me begin with a cinematic parable. In a movie called *Executive Decision*, a terrorist group hijacks a Boeing 747 commercial jet and flies it to Washington, D.C., where they plan to explode a bomb filled with deadly nerve gas. Considering that the movie was made in 1996, it is eerily prophetic.

The plane, if you will allow the comparison, is like God's creation. God's creation is good. It was launched by God to be a joyful journey toward a glorious destination. But along the way it was hijacked. Sin came into the world, because some of the passengers decided to take over the plane and fly it to their own destination, instead of the destination that God intended. So now the plane is headed for destruction, not only the destruction of the passengers but the destruction of God's whole creation.

What will God do about this? In the movie the U.S. military tries various ways to deal with the situation. They try negotiating with the terrorists, but the terrorists will not be dissuaded. Then the military sends fighter jets to divert

65

the plane to a safe landing site, but the terrorists ignore them and continue on their destructive course.

It is like the law and the prophets in the Bible. God sends the Ten Commandments, trying to help us understand that if we continue in sin and rebellion, we will destroy ourselves and everything else. Then God sends the prophets, like fighter jets, to turn us around and direct us to a safe landing, but we don't listen.

One reason we don't listen is that like the passengers on the plane we are trapped. In Romans 7 the apostle Paul says, "For we know that the law is spiritual; but I am of the flesh sold into slavery under sin. I do not understand my own actions. For I do not do what I want, but I do the very thing that I hate" (Romans 7:14-15).

When we allow sin to have its way in our lives, it is like terrorists taking over the plane. We become captives and lose the ability to turn the plane around by ourselves. We are trapped on an airplane headed for destruction, and the only way to stop it is by shooting it down, destroying the passengers in the process.

But then someone comes up with a wild idea. They send an anti-terrorist assault team to board the plane in mid-air. They fly the team out in a Stealth bomber, approaching the jet from behind and underneath where it cannot be seen from the cockpit or the windows. Then in mid-air they attach a docking collar to a hatch under the plane, and the assault team climbs through the docking collar into the cargo hold of the jet without the terrorists knowing it.

Here is where we get to Jesus. None of the passengers inside the plane have the power to save themselves. They do not have the weapons to overcome the terrorists or the skill to diffuse the bomb. They must be saved by someone more powerful coming into the plane from the outside. Someone must enter their world—their captivity—and liberate them from the inside.

For me this is an image of what Christians call the incarnation. The incarnation is when Jesus boards the plane, when Jesus enters our world of captivity to sin and death. All the efforts to change us from the outside failed. God tried to reason with us through the commandments and sent prophets, like fighter jets, to divert us. But these things failed to turn the plane around. We could not be saved from the outside; we had to be saved from the inside. Jesus had to enter our world in order to defeat the power of sin—to defuse the bomb ticking inside of us and turn the plane around, taking us where we were meant to go all along.

God in Person

When my youngest son was five years old, we had a conversation in the car, the kind of conversation a parent never forgets. We were riding along when suddenly he turned to me and said, "God is bigger than you, isn't he Dad?" "Yes," I said, pleased that he was thinking about God, "God is bigger than me." He was quiet for a minute, then he said, "God's nicer than you, too, isn't he, Dad?" I was not sure where this conversation was going, but I said, "Yes, God is nicer than me." Again he was quiet for a minute, then he said, "Jesus is nicer than you, too, huh Dad?" I wondered how low I would go on the nice scale, but I said, "Yes, Jesus is nicer than me." "Yeah," he concluded, "Jesus and God are the same nice."

That is not a bad understanding of the Christian faith. It highlights two important points:

1. Our "niceness" does not always measure up. My son had a front row seat to my flaws. He had seen me get impatient and not pay attention to him, and sometimes treat him unfairly. Thankfully he knew that God is nicer than me.
2. Jesus and God are the same nice. My son could not have articulated the theology behind this, but even at his young age he sensed that in Jesus we are meeting the love of God in person, and that makes all the difference.

In his book *Credo*, William Sloane Coffin says,

Jesus is both a mirror to our humanity and a window to divinity, a window revealing as much of God as is given mortal eyes to see. When Christians see Christ empowering the weak, scorning the powerful, healing the wounded, and judging their tormentors, we are seeing transparently the power of God at work. What is finally important is not that Christ is Godlike, but that God is Christ-like. God is like Christ.[1]

At the heart of the Christian faith is the belief that a personal God has entered our world in person to make us new persons. We believe that God came to us in Jesus to redeem the world.

Shocking Claims

Interestingly, Jesus is popular even among those who do not believe he is God's Son. Mohammed was clear about recognizing Jesus as a prophet. Many others extol him as a great teacher. Some of Jesus' teachings are found in other religions, such as the Golden Rule: "In everything do to others as you would have them do to you" (Matthew 7:12). Buddhists have always liked Jesus' teaching about worry: "So do not worry about tomorrow, for tomorrow will bring worries of its own. Today's trouble is enough for today" (Matthew 6:34).

But these are not the kind of statements that would have gotten someone crucified. What alarmed both the Roman governor and the Jewish leaders was the authority Jesus claimed for himself.

In one story some friends bring a paralyzed man to Jesus on a stretcher (Mark 2:1-12). When they cannot get to Jesus because of the crowd around the door, they carry the stretcher on top of the house, remove part of the roof, and let the man down in front of Jesus with ropes. It is an impressive effort. Seeing their faith, Jesus says to the paralyzed man, "Son, your sins are forgiven."

I doubt that forgiveness is what the paralyzed man or his friends had in mind. They were looking for healing. But the Jewish religious leaders were appalled by Jesus' claim. They say to themselves, "Why does this fellow speak in this way? It is blasphemy! Who can forgive sins but God alone?"

Good question. If you run a stop sign and smash into my car, I have the right to forgive you, as long as I pay for the damage and do not submit a claim to my insurance company. But what right do I have to forgive you for smashing someone else's car?

Jesus claims the authority to forgive *all* of the paralyzed man's sins—not just any wrong he might have done to Jesus, but any wrong he might have done to anyone. Who can do that except God?

Knowing what they are thinking, Jesus says to the Jewish leaders, "Why do you raise such questions in your hearts? Which is easier, to say to the paralytic, 'Your sins are forgiven,' or to say, 'Stand up and take your mat and walk'?"

Another good question. In one sense it is easier to say, "Your sins are forgiven," because who could prove you wrong? But in another sense forgiving sin is the harder thing to do. Which is easier to heal: a broken leg or a broken heart?

Without waiting for an answer Jesus says to the paralyzed man, "I say to you, stand up, take your mat and go to your home," and the paralyzed man does so.

The story shows a recurring pattern in Jesus' ministry. Jesus does the easier visible action to show his authority to do something harder and invisible. He heals the paralyzed man to show that he can also forgive sins. He opens the eyes of the blind to show that he is the light of the world. He feeds 5000 people with five loaves of bread to show that he is the bread of life, and he raises Lazarus from the dead to show that he is the resurrection and the life for all.

To regard Jesus as just another great teacher, like Mohammed or Buddha, does not do him justice. Once when his disciples were picking grains of wheat and eating them on the Sabbath, the Jewish leaders accused Jesus of breaking God's commandment against working on the Sabbath. Had Jesus said, "Oh, come on, quit making such a big deal of trivial matters," many of his Jewish contemporaries would have nodded agreement. But instead he says, "The Sabbath was made for humankind, and not humankind for the Sabbath." Then he adds, "The Son of Man [meaning himself] is lord of the Sabbath" (Mark 2:27-28).

Wait a minute. The Sabbath was God's commandment. Who does Jesus think he is, claiming to be "lord" of the Sabbath?

On another occasion Jesus and his disciples are crossing the Sea of Galilee when a storm threatens to swamp their boat. Jesus rebukes the wind and says to the sea, "Peace! Be still!" And the storm ceases (Mark 4:39). The last time someone commanded the sea by a mere word, it was God at the creation (Genesis 1:9). This is not lost on the disciples. They say to one another, "Who then is this, that even the wind and sea obey him?" (Mark 4:41).

Finally, at his trial the high priest confronts Jesus over claims that he is the Messiah. The high priest asks, "Are you the Messiah, the Son of the Blessed One?" Jesus replies, "I am." Then he takes his response to another level: "And you will see the Son of Man [meaning himself] seated at the right hand of the Power [meaning God] and coming with the clouds of heaven" (Mark 14:62).

It was not his sensible teaching that led to Jesus' execution. It was his audacious claim to be the Son of God, acting and speaking as if he were God.

For me this is the most important thing about Jesus. It means that when Jesus forgives people, God is forgiving them, and that includes me. And when Jesus shows compassion for hungry people, either physically hungry or spiritually hungry, it means that God is concerned about them, and that I should be too. And when the judgment comes, standing at the right hand of God will be not my accuser but my Savior, and that gives me hope.

Vindication

By all rights the Christian faith should not have survived Jesus' death. This is not the case with other religions. Most great world religions have had no trouble surviving the death of their founder. Confucius, Buddha, and Mohammed were all considered great teachers or prophets, which meant that their followers could hold on to their teachings even after they died. Albert Einstein may have originated the Theory of Relativity, but that theory does not depend on

Albert Einstein for its truth. It is valid whether Einstein is alive or not.

Not so with Christianity. The disciples did not follow Jesus only because of his teaching. They were impressed by his teaching, to be sure, but what amazed them was the authority he claimed for himself. He claimed to be the Messiah, the Christ, God's chosen king to bring God's righteousness and peace to the world. The disciples believed this was true. Such a belief should not have survived the crucifixion.

In 132 A.D. a man named Simon Bar Kokba led a Jewish revolt against the Romans. At first he had so much success he proclaimed himself to be the Messiah and attracted thousands of followers. Three years later he was killed, and overnight his movement vanished.

By all rights the same thing should have happened to Jesus. When Jesus died on the cross, all faith in him should have been shattered.

And at first it was shattered. In Luke 24 the disciples are told about the resurrection, and verse 11 says, "These words seemed to them an idle tale, and they did not believe them." Later in the same chapter two of his disciples trudge away from Jerusalem toward the town of Emmaus. They encounter a stranger who turns out to be Jesus, but they do not recognize him, partly because they are not expecting to see him. The stranger asks what they are discussing, and they tell him about what happened to Jesus, concluding, "But we had hoped that he was the one to redeem Israel" (Luke 24:21). You can hear the disappointment in their words. Even when told that his body is missing from the tomb, neither of them jumps to the conclusion that he is risen from the dead.

In John's gospel Mary goes to the tomb and finds it empty. She assumes that someone has taken away the body. It never occurs to her that Jesus is risen from the dead. Even when she sees him, she mistakes him for the gardener, and she asks where he has taken the body. When Jesus dies on the cross, so does the disciples' faith in him.

And then, somehow, it is reborn. Somehow this discouraged, disillusioned group of disciples became the most fearless missionaries the world had ever seen. One minute they are puzzling over an empty tomb, and the next minute they are preaching courageously all over the Mediterranean. And their message is that Jesus is alive.

At times it has been difficult for me to believe in Jesus' resurrection. After all, I have not seen it for myself. I must rely on the testimony of those who claimed to have seen him. And how do I know they were not imagining things, or deluding themselves?

And yet I keep coming back to two indisputable facts of history: 1) that Jesus was executed by Pontius Pilate, a fact attested even in sources outside the Bible, and 2) that his followers continued to believe in him. And they believed not only that he was a great teacher, a powerful prophet, or a wise sage, but that he was the Risen Lord, the promised king, the Messiah, who would bring God's righteousness and peace to the world.

Something happened between Good Friday and Pentecost, and that something is Easter. The disciples believed in Jesus not because they liked his teaching or his politics, but because they met him risen from the dead. It was not his principles but his presence—his living presence—that changed their lives forever.

Jesus' resurrection vindicated his claim. God would not have raised from the dead a person guilty of blasphemy. By raising Jesus from the dead, God set a seal of approval on Jesus. The apostle Paul later said of Jesus, "[He] was descended from David according to the flesh and was declared to be Son of God with power according to the spirit of holiness by resurrection from the dead" (Romans 1:3-4). The resurrection vindicated Jesus' claim of authority to forgive sins, and it demonstrated his power to transform lives even beyond the grave.

It also vindicated God's intention for creation. As noted in chapter 2, Jesus' resurrection was not a case of his soul rising through a tunnel of light to be with God while his body decayed in the tomb. The tomb was empty. All four gospels insist on that point. God raised Jesus' body from the dead, thereby declaring God's intention to transform bodily life, to end the curse that had hung over creation since Genesis 3.

This is part of the answer to my friend Mike's question: How can a good and powerful God allow evil in the world? In high school I did not know how to answer that question. I am still not sure I know the whole answer. But believing in Jesus' resurrection, as his first followers clearly did, means believing God is not finished with us yet. There is hope for what God will yet do to change the world. The prophet Isaiah imagined this future for the world:

> On this mountain the LORD of hosts will make for all
>   peoples
> a feast of rich food, a feast of well-aged wines,
> of rich food filled with marrow, of well-aged wines
>   strained clear.
> And he will destroy on this mountain
> the shroud that is cast over all peoples,
> the sheet that is spread over all nations;
> he will swallow up death forever.
> Then the Lord GOD will wipe away the tears from all
>   faces,
> and the disgrace of his people he will take away from
>   all the earth,
> for the LORD has spoken" (Isaiah 25:6-8).

Jesus' resurrection was God's first installment on that promise.

But Why Did He Die?

But this raises a puzzling question: why did Jesus die? If God could raise Jesus from the dead, why didn't God prevent his death in the first place?

At this point I think the disciples remembered the Last Supper. On the night before his death, Jesus sat at a table with them to celebrate the Passover. Taking the bread and breaking it, he said, "This is my body that is for you. Do this in remembrance of me" (I Corinthians 11:24). Knowing that his death was close at hand, Jesus wanted his disciples to understand its meaning. He was giving his body for them—for us!

This is confirmed by what Jesus says next as he passes the cup of wine. He says, "This cup is the new covenant in my blood. Do this, as often as you drink it, in remembrance of me" (I Corinthians 11:25). The reference to his blood is clearly a reference to his death. Jesus wants the disciples to know that his death opens the door to a new relationship with God, a new covenant made possible by his sacrifice.

In many ways this is the deepest and hardest Christian belief to explain. I remember a person from my church in Spokane challenging me on this. How does Jesus' unjust death do anything for us? And why would God need to see some blood before saving us?

The Bible uses different images to capture the idea. The apostle Paul describes it as an atoning sacrifice, like the sacrifices offered in the Old Testament temple. He says, "For there is no distinction, since all have sinned and fall short of the glory of God; they are now justified by his grace as a gift, through the redemption that is in Christ Jesus, whom God put forward as a sacrifice of atonement by his blood, effective through faith" (Romans 3:22b-25a).

Jesus himself calls it a ransom, like the payment to rescue a hostage or release a slave. He says, "For the Son of Man came not to be served but to serve, and to give his life a ransom for many" (Mark 10:45).

While helpful to Christians in many times and places, neither of these images has been particularly helpful to me. But it has been helpful for me to think about what gives Jesus the right to forgive us. Earlier in the chapter we looked at Jesus' shocking claim of authority to forgive all sins. We might accept Jesus' authority to forgive the wrongs done to *him*, but what gives him the right to forgive all the wrongs we have done to others?

After the shootings at an African Methodist Episcopal Church in Charleston, South Carolina, family members of the victims confronted the shooter, Dylan Roof, at his initial court hearing. But instead of angry calls for his rapid consignment to hell, they offered words of forgiveness and prayers for

God's mercy. "I forgive you, my family forgives you," said Anthony Thompson, whose wife was killed in the attack. Nadine Collier, the daughter of another shooting victim told him, "You took something very precious away from me. I will never talk to her again. I will never be able to hold her again. But I forgive you. And [may God] have mercy on your soul."[2]

These are powerful expressions of forgiveness from people deeply injured by Dylan Roof's actions. But how would we have felt if the judge in the case had said to Dylan Roof, "I forgive you; case dismissed"? We would be outraged. Our sense of justice would be deeply violated, especially since the judge was not one of the people who lost a family member.

Serious wrongs cannot be forgiven by a wave of the hand, even by God. If God forgave all the evil in the world with a mere wave of the hand, a deep sense of injustice would still prevail. Evil causes real damage to God's beloved children and God's beloved creation, and only the person who shares in the suffering has the right to forgive it.

Which, we believe, is what Jesus did on the cross. A transcendent God could not share in the suffering caused by human evil, but an incarnate God could. On the cross Jesus paid the price for all the damage we have done to others and to God's creation. In a way that we can never fully explain, Jesus took on himself all the consequences of our wrongdoing.

As the disciples pondered this, their minds turned to the puzzling portrait of a suffering servant in the prophecies of Isaiah.

> But he was wounded for our transgressions, crushed for our iniquities; upon him was the punishment that made us whole, and by his bruises we are healed. All we like sheep have gone astray; we have all turned to our own way, and the Lord has laid on him the iniquity of us all (Isaiah 53:5-6).

My own analogy for Jesus' death is the image of lead rods in a nuclear reactor. In a nuclear reaction, or at least in a fission reaction, atoms are smashed by particles hitting them at high speed. When the atoms break apart, they release energy, but they also release more atomic particles that smash into other atoms and release more energy in an ever expanding chain reaction. This serves as a picture for the ripple effect of sin noted in connection with Genesis 3.

But if sin is like a nuclear reaction, then Jesus is like the lead rods in the reactor. Engineers use rods made of lead to stop the reaction, because lead absorbs the flying atomic particles without splitting and sending out more particles. Lead rods stop a nuclear reaction by absorbing the damage instead of passing it along.

When applied to Jesus we call this the atonement. When Jesus died on the cross, instead of passing on the flying particles of hurt and injustice in the world, he took them into himself. He absorbed in himself the destructive consequences of wrongdoing so that the cycle of injury and retaliation could finally be stopped.

But there is an even deeper side to the story. At the heart of our meaning as human beings is a relationship to God. We were created in the image of God so we could be capable of such a relationship. But wrongdoing not only damages our relationships to others, it damages our relationship to God. Jesus' death on the cross not only pays for the damage but repairs the broken relationship. The apostle Paul describes it this way:

> But God proves his love for us in that while we still were sinners Christ died for us. Much more surely then, now that we have been justified by his blood, will we be saved through him from the wrath of God. For if while we were enemies, we were reconciled to God through the death of his Son, much more surely, having been reconciled, will we be saved by his life (Romans 5:8-10).

Again I cannot explain how or why this works. But when the first followers of Jesus reflected on the deep truth that Jesus died for them, they realized Jesus' love in a way they had never before understood. And since Jesus embodied the truth about God, they also experienced the love God had for them—a love that transformed their lives.

God and Child Abuse

During a continuing education event at a seminary, I had dinner with a student who said to me, "Isn't the idea of God sending his Son to die for us on a cross a case of child abuse?" I said, "What?" He said, "Well, if God sacrificed his Son for us on a cross, wasn't God in effect abusing his own child?"

It had never occurred to me to think of it this way. I had always understood Jesus' sacrifice on the cross as a good thing. Isn't that why we call it "Good Friday"? God sent his Son and allowed him to die on the cross in order to save us. But here was a seminary student suggesting we report God to Child Protective Services.

Actually, it is not just Jesus' death which creates a problem for us with God. Every child that is hurt or abused calls into question God's goodness. In Dostoyevsky's novel *The Brothers Karamazov*, there is a scene where Ivan, a morose agnostic, confronts his devout brother Alyosha about atrocities committed against Russian children. Ivan says,

> I've collected a great, great deal about Russian children, Alyosha. There was a little girl of five who was hated by her father and mother, 'most worthy and respectable people, of good education and breeding.' ... This poor child of five was subjected to every possible torture by those cultivated parents. They beat her, kicked her for no reason till her body was one bruise. Then they went to greater refinements of cruelty— shut her up all night in the cold and frost in a privy, because she [wet her bed at night]. Can you understand why a little creature, who can't even understand what's done to her, should beat her little aching heart with her tiny fist in the dark and cold, and weep her meek unresentful tears to dear, kind God to protect her? Do you understand that, Alyosha? Do you understand why this infamy must be and is permitted?[3]

You need not read a Russian novel to find cases of child abuse. Why does God allow children to suffer? Isn't the suffering of even one child—any child—a case of divine child abuse?

But what if God is not only the Father but the child? What if God is not only the Creator who gave us the freedom to sin, but also the creature who suffers the consequences of it?

Thinking about it this way gave me a new understanding of the incarnation. Colossians 1:19-20 says of Jesus, "In him all the fullness of God was pleased to dwell, and through him God was pleased to reconcile to himself all things, whether on earth or in heaven, by making peace through the blood of his cross."

If God had sent someone else to die for us, if God had appointed some other innocent person to suffer for our sins, then we could question God's love, as the seminary student did. But what if God is not only the Father but the Son? What if God was in Christ dying for us on that cross? What if all the fullness of God was present in Jesus as he suffered to save us? What if God was the sacrifice?

In a book called *Night*, Elie Wiesel, a holocaust survivor, tells about an experience in the Nazi concentration camp at Auschwitz:

> One day, as we returned from work, we saw three gallows, ... three prisoners in chains—and among them [a young boy]. ... The three condemned prisoners together stepped onto the chairs. In unison, the nooses were placed around their necks. ... "Where is merciful God, where is He?" someone behind me was asking. At the signal, the three chairs were tipped over. Total silence in the camp. On the horizon, the sun was setting. ... Then came the march past the victims. The two men were no longer alive. ... But the third rope was still moving: the child, too light, was still breathing ... Behind me, I heard the same man asking: "For God's sake, where is God?" And from within me, I heard a voice answer: "Where is He? This is where—hanging here from this gallows."[4]

For Christians, that is the deepest meaning of the incarnation. The whole world is a case of divine child abuse, unless God is not only the Father but the Child, not only the Creator but the one who suffers for all the horrible ways we have misused our created freedom. Almost all religions believe in a god who punishes evil. Only the Bible pictures a God who suffers for it, and therefore has the right to forgive it.

Jesus and Other Religions

C. S. Lewis once pointed out that only atheists have to believe that all other religions are completely mistaken. Christians are free to recognize that all religions, even those very different from ours, may contain some echoes of the truth, some fingerprints of God.[5]

As noted earlier, there are many similarities in the ethical teachings of Jesus and those in other religions. There are also many of the same yearnings for the healing of our world. This should not surprise us since Christians believe in one God who created all the peoples of the earth.

But in most if not all other religions, human work is a key component to achieving the life God wants us to have. At the center of Judaism is the Torah—God's law. At the center of Buddhism are the ten noble truths which describe the actions and attitudes needed to reach Nirvana. At the center of Islam is the Qur'an, the revelation of what we need to do to get to heaven.

But at the center of Christianity is a cross. To be sure there are also commandments of God in the Bible, which includes the Jewish Torah. There are also teachings of Jesus and of the apostles, some of which lay out the kind of life and actions consistent with God's coming kingdom. But at the heart of the Christian faith is not a teacher like Moses, Mohammed, or Buddha. At the heart of the Christian faith is someone who dies for us on a cross to give us a relationship with God that we cannot earn.

While the Qur'an calls Jesus a prophet and urges people to honor his teaching, Mohammed did not believe that Jesus really died on the cross. The Qur'an says of Jesus, "They did not kill him, nor did they crucify him, though it was made to appear like that to them; ... they certainly did not kill him—God raised him up to Himself."[6] The Qur'an skips the cross and goes straight to the ascension.

But for Christians the cross is the heart of the story. The apostle Paul says to the church in Corinth, "When I came to you, brothers and sisters, I did not come proclaiming the mystery of God to you in lofty words or wisdom. For I decided to know nothing among you except Jesus Christ, and him crucified" (I Corinthians 2:2). For Paul the cross is central to the Christian faith because it screams as loudly as possible the idea that we are saved by grace, not by following certain commandments or teachings. If we could be saved by the teachings of Jesus or anyone else, Jesus would not have needed to die on the cross. But the fact that he did, the fact that God allowed it to happen, means we could not save ourselves by any form of teaching, nor any list of commandments or noble truths. We are saved for a personal relationship with God only by God's personal intervention on our behalf. As Paul says, "For the message about the cross is foolishness to those who are perishing, but to us who are being saved it is the power of God" (I Corinthians 1:18).

Those were not the words of a dissolute drunk who hit bottom. Those were the words of the apostle Paul, a well-educated, devout, scrupulously obedient student of the Torah, who realized that his works-based righteousness had only fed his false pride, alienating him from the relationship with God for which he was created.

This does not mean that the commandments of God or the teachings of Jesus are no longer relevant to us as Christians. Rather they take on a different meaning in light of God's grace shown to us in Jesus. And that will be the subject of the next chapter.

Questions for Discussion

1. How would you describe Jesus to someone who had never heard of him and knew nothing about him? What would you emphasize about him or his story?

2. What does the Easter story mean to you? What for you is the meaning or significance of the claim that Jesus is risen from the dead?
3. How would you interpret the statement "Jesus saves"? Saves from what? Saves how?
4. How do you see Christian beliefs similar to or different from other religions?

Grace, Relationship, and Transformation

In previous chapters I have shared some of the struggles I had with guilt, feeling even as a child that I was not good enough for God. I shared in chapter 3 about reading a biography of Martin Luther and discovering the idea of grace—that God accepts us not because we are good enough but because God loves us and demonstrated that love through Jesus, who died and rose from the dead to make us part of God's family forever. For me grace produced gratitude, and gratitude produced a new desire to serve God, not out of fear but out of hope that God might use me to do good in the world. This connection between grace, gratitude, and new possibilities for life will be the theme of this chapter. But first I must explain a distinction, often misunderstood, between forgiveness and grace.

Grace Beyond Forgiveness

At a forum on world religions held in our church, an Islamic speaker gave a spirited explanation of Islam, emphasizing that it is not a religion of coercion, but a religion of free choice. He said that people can choose to worship God and obey God's commands in the Qur'an, or they can reject God and follow a path that takes them away from God.

During the question and answer time I asked, "What about grace? Is there a place for grace in Islam?" "Absolutely," he said. "Allah is a God of mercy. If we do wrong and ask forgiveness, Allah will accept us."

I noticed that he answered my question about grace with a comment about forgiveness. But are they the same?

It is not uncommon to equate the two. In this view grace is like a second chance, something you get when you say you are sorry. If you repent of the wrongs you have done and turn back to God, God will forgive you and accept you.

But that is not always how Jesus approached it. Passing through Jericho, Jesus met a Jewish tax collector named Zacchaeus. The Romans franchised the business of collecting taxes. Each tax collector had to remit a certain amount of money to the Romans. Anything they collected over that amount they could keep for themselves. Zacchaeus, we are told, was rich, which probably meant that in some way he coerced people into paying more taxes than the Romans required, possibly by threatening to report them to the Romans as tax evaders. Zacchaeus was less like a county assessor and more like a mafia boss running a protection racket.

But out of all the people in Jericho who crowded the roads that day, Jesus chose Zacchaeus for a personal visit. He said to him, "Zacchaeus"—calling him by name suggests that Jesus knows all about Zacchaeus and his profession—"hurry and come down, for I must stay at your house today" (Luke 19:5).

Did we miss something? Did Zacchaeus repent before Jesus graced him with his presence? Did Zacchaeus cry out from the sycamore tree, "Lord, have mercy on me a sinner"? Did Zacchaeus admit that he had done anything wrong or promise to change? No. Jesus came to Zacchaeus' home and into Zacchaeus' life *before* he repented, before he did a single thing to admit his guilt or change his ways.

I don't think our speaker on Islam would have gone along with Jesus on this. Nor did the Jewish people in Jericho. They were not opposed to forgiveness. What bothered the people of Jericho is that Jesus accepted Zacchaeus before he repented—before he showed any remorse, made any restitution, or did anything else to turn his life around.

Jesus did this often. In Luke 15:1-2 we read, "Now all the tax collectors and sinners were coming near to listen to Jesus. And the Pharisees and scribes were grumbling and saying, 'This fellow welcomes sinners and eats with them.'" The Pharisees and scribes were not opposed to God's forgiveness. They were glad to welcome repentant sinners. But they were scandalized that Jesus accepted known sinners into his fellowship without preconditions—without first requiring remorse, repentance, and a recognition of their need for forgiveness.

Jesus responds to their criticism with a parable about a shepherd who leaves his ninety-nine sheep in the wilderness and goes looking for the one that is lost. When he finds it, he puts it on his shoulders and brings it home rejoicing (Luke 15:3-7).

Did the sheep ever say it was sorry? Did the sheep ask the shepherd's forgiveness and promise never to do it again? No. The shepherd shows grace to the sheep before the sheep does anything to repent of its errant ways.

Of course sheep cannot repent, which means that this may not be the best illustration. So Jesus moves on to a different example: "There was a man who had two sons. The younger of them said to his father, 'Father, give me the share of the property that will belong to me'" (Luke 15:11-12). In effect he is telling his father, "I'm tired of waiting for you to die. Give me my inheritance now." So the father gives him his inheritance, and the son goes off to a far country and squanders it.

Now he is in trouble. He has no money and nothing to eat. So he decides to go back to his father because he figures that even his father's hired hands have it better than he does. On the way he practices his speech: "Father, I have sinned against heaven and before you; I am no longer worthy to be called your son; treat me like one of your hired hands" (Luke 15:18-19). As a hired hand, the prodigal is not only planning to get shelter and provision from his father, but possibly to pay back the portion of the inheritance he squandered.[1]

At this point the Pharisees and scribes would have agreed with this parable. So would the Islamic speaker. A prodigal son realizes the error of his ways and goes back to his father, expressing remorse and offering to make restitution. That is how it is supposed to work. If you repent and return to God, God will forgive you.

The surprise comes in verse 20: "But while he was still far off, his father saw him and was filled with compassion; he ran and put his arms around him and kissed him." The father goes out of his way to show love and acceptance for his son before the son has a chance to admit his sin or promise restitution.

As I noted when this parable was discussed in chapter 1, the father is not concerned about money but relationship. The relationship was broken by the son thinking that the father's money was more important than the father. Thus it cannot be restored by the son thinking he can pay back the father with labor. The relationship can only be restored 1) when the father shows the depth of his love for his son by conferring on him the gifts of "sonship" (robe, ring, and party), and 2) when the son accepts these gifts and returns to the father's home and family. In other words, reconciliation hinges not on making amends but on giving and accepting grace.

Interestingly, the father goes through the same thing with the older son, the supposedly dutiful one. The older son's refusal to come to the party is itself dishonoring to the father, and indicative of a broken relationship. But once again the father takes the initiative, going out to the rebellious older brother and begging him to come to the party. In the ethos of that culture the father humiliates himself twice: first in throwing a party for a dissolute prodigal, then in having to leave the party and go outside to persuade his older brother to join the celebration.[2]

To be sure, Jesus assumes a need for repentance by those who would come to the Father. His first sermon in both Matthew and Mark begins with the word "repent." On numerous occasions Jesus emphasizes that a relationship with God requires a new set of attitudes and behavior toward God and one another. But for Jesus, repentance is not a condition of God's grace; it is a consequence of it.

We see this in the case of Zacchaeus. After Jesus comes to his house Zacchaeus says, "Half of my possessions I will give to the poor; and if I have defrauded anyone of anything I will pay back four times as much." Zacchaeus speaks these words *after* his acceptance by Jesus, not before. The change in Zacchaeus does not earn him grace; rather grace prompts the change in Zacchaeus.

In the Christian faith the healing of our broken lives and broken relationships begins not with us but with Jesus. Grace means that Jesus accepts us as we are, and that acceptance becomes the first step in Jesus' transforming work in our lives.

A Case Study in Grace

In 1995 when Larry Whitson arrived at the Union Gospel Mission in Spokane, his clothes were still damp from a suicide attempt. Overwhelmed by depression over a broken marriage, and feeling guilt for a crime he never confessed, Larry jumped off a bridge into the Spokane River. But instead of drowning, the current spit him out on a sandy beach, sort of like the Biblical Jonah. After that, Larry walked aimlessly across town, his clothes dripping wet, until he came to the Union Gospel Mission. He was greeted by a resident of the Mission who asked why he was there. Larry told him the dark secrets of his past, things he had never shared with anyone else. He was certain the man would despise him for what he had done, but the man said to him, "A month ago I would've called you scum, but today I understand God's love differently, and I can call you my brother."

As Larry began to experience God's grace—God's unconditional acceptance—he realized what he had to do. He turned himself in to the Spokane Police and made a full confession of his crime. As a result, he was sentenced to eight months in prison. Even when God forgives us, we must still face some of the consequences of our actions. But those consequences do not have the last word. When Larry got out of prison he returned to the Mission and joined their Life Regeneration Program. He has since found a job and a home, and has begun a Bible study in his neighborhood. Then he wrote a poem called "Bruised Reed" based on Isaiah 42.

There was a time my life was like a reed which had
    been bruised
Tormented by the childhood wounds I suffered
    through abuse;
And there were those who often said my worthless life
    was lost
Too bad, they said, but what's the use, it's such a
    helpless cause.

Adulthood came and true to form, expectancy fulfilled,
My stone cold heart and darkened soul brought forth a
    stubborn will
The reed became smoldering flax that stank for all to see
Abandoned now by all I knew there seemed no hope
    for me.

But Jesus Christ will never break a reed that has been
    bruised
And never will He quench a flax that smolders from
    abuse;
He has a purpose all his own for everything he does
But when it comes to you and me, he loves us just
    because…

Blind eyes are made to see again, deaf ears are made to
    hear,
A cold and stony, darkened heart turns soft when love
    appears;
And Jesus helps us most of all through warmth of love
    He brings
Though undeserving, His embrace has healing in its
    wings.[3]

In all of these stories the order is not 1) repentance, 2)
grace, and 3) relationship. It is 1) grace, 2) relationship, and
3) transformation.

Might this suggest, however, that grace is still
conditional—that grace can be lost if transformation does
not follow from it?

Grace and New Life

There is a case to be made that Michael Phelps is the greatest Olympic swimmer of all time, but for me his greatest performance was at the 2004 Olympics in a race he did not swim.

That year on his way to six gold medals Michael Phelps did something almost unthinkable. He gave up his spot in the finals of the 4X100 medley relay to another member of the American team, a butterfly swimmer named Ian Crocker. He did this so that Crocker would have the chance to win a gold medal.

This was an act of grace. Ian Crocker did not earn his place on that relay team. By all rights Michael Phelps should have been swimming the butterfly leg of the race. The day before, Phelps had won the gold medal in the 100-meter butterfly, beating Ian Crocker among others. But Phelps wanted Ian Crocker to experience the thrill of winning a gold medal in the Olympics, so he sacrificed his place on the team so that Crocker could compete.

The parallel to Jesus seems obvious. Jesus sacrificed himself so that we could have a place in God's kingdom. That is what Christians call grace. It is not something we earn. It is a gift given to us by Jesus' sacrifice.

But what if, given that opportunity, Ian Crocker had said, "Oh, I don't want to swim; I just want to march in the opening ceremony and wear one of those cool warm-ups while hanging out with the other athletes in the Olympic village"?

Had Ian Crocker done that, he would have missed out on the point of Michael Phelps' sacrifice. He would have missed the thrill of being on a gold medal team.

When Michael Phelps gave Ian Crocker his spot on the team, Crocker could have said, "No, thanks. I am not good enough; I don't want that kind of responsibility." He could have run away, fearing that he would mess up the race for the entire team. But he didn't. Instead, the next day he went out and swam the race of his life. Not only did his team win the gold medal, but they broke the world record. One day Ian Crocker wasn't even on the team. The next day he was standing on the gold medal platform with his name next to a world record.

In Romans 6, the apostle Paul says, "What then are we to say? Should we continue in sin in order that grace may abound? By no means! How can we who died to sin go on living in it?" (Romans 6:1-2). Having been given a new life in Christ with forgiveness, acceptance, purpose, and hope, Paul cannot imagine why anyone would want to throw that away. Later in the same chapter Paul says,

> When you were slaves of sin, you were free in regard to righteousness. So what advantage did you then get from the things of which you are now ashamed? The end of those things is death. But now that you have been freed from sin and enslaved to God, the advantage you get is sanctification. The end is eternal life (Romans 6:20-22).

The Heidelberg Catechism, one of the confessions of the Presbyterian Church (USA), asks this question: "Since we have been delivered from our misery by grace through Christ without any merit of our own, why then should we do good works?" Answer:

> Because Christ, having redeemed us by his blood, is also restoring us by his Spirit into his image, so that with our whole lives we may show that we are thankful to God for his benefits, so that he may be praised through us, so that we may be assured of our faith by its fruits, and so that by our godly living our neighbors may be won over to Christ.[4]

The motive for good works in the Christian life is not fear of punishment but gratitude for grace, combined with a desire to share that grace with others.

The Structure of Love

Why then did God give us commandments to obey? Not because the commandments are a condition of salvation, but because the commandments show us what salvation is like. They are the structure of love.

Before giving the Ten Commandments, the Lord said to Moses, "You have seen what I did to the Egyptians, and how I bore you on eagles' wings and brought you to myself" (Exodus 19:4). This refers to the story of the exodus—how God freed the Israelites from slavery in Egypt and parted the waters of the Red Sea so they could escape. The Ten Commandments were not given as requirements to pass in order to be saved. The Israelites had already been saved. They had already been set free. The commandments were snapshots of how this new life of freedom was supposed to look.

God tells us not to have other gods—whether it is money, sports, career, possessions, or status—because sooner or later they will disappoint us. They will let us down, and God wants something better for us.

The same is true with the other commandments. God tells us to keep the Sabbath, because there is more to life than work. God tells us not to commit adultery, because there is more to life than sex. God tells us not to covet because there is more to life than keeping up with the neighbors. God prohibits these things not to stifle us, but to set us free for something better. The Ten Commandments are a guide not only to our own blessing but for making us a blessing to others.

In his *Small Catechism*, Martin Luther gives a striking explanation for each of the Ten Commandments.[5] Even though most of the commandments are worded in the negative—don't do this, don't do that—Luther gives each of them a positive spin. For example, when discussing the commandment "You shall not kill," Luther says, "We should fear and love God, and so we should not endanger our neighbor's life, nor cause him any harm, *but help and befriend him in every necessity of life*" (my emphasis). Suddenly the commandment against murder has become a mission statement. Hunger relief, shelter for the homeless, medical care, feeding and caring for children—all these things are wrapped up in this commandment. It is not just about avoiding murder; it is about serving one another in love.

Luther does the same with the next commandment: "You shall not commit adultery." He says, "We should fear and love God, and so *we should lead a chaste and pure life in word and deed, each one loving and honoring his wife or husband*" (my emphasis). Marriage is not just about avoiding an affair. It is about a mission God gives us to love and care for our spouse.

My favorite is Luther's explanation for the commandment "You shall not bear false witness against your neighbor." He begins with the obvious: "We should not tell lies about our neighbor, nor betray, slander, or defame him." But then he goes a step further: "But (we) should apologize for him, speak well of him, and interpret charitably all that he does." Imagine if instead of condemning people or making fun of them, we tried to explain their actions in the kindest way possible. That does not mean agreeing with them or condoning anything they do. But it may soften our attitude toward other people as we try to understand the situations or life experiences behind their words and actions.

Jesus was once asked, "Which is the greatest commandment?" He replied, "You shall love the Lord your God with all your heart, and with all your soul, and with all your mind. ... And a second is like it: You shall love your neighbor as yourself" (Matthew 22:37-39).

Some might conclude from this that we don't need the commandments. To quote the Beatles, "All you need is love." But Jesus did not say that. Earlier in Matthew's gospel Jesus says, "Do not think I have come to abolish the law and the prophets. I have not come to abolish but to fulfill" (Matthew 5:17). The Ten Commandments are not superfluous to love. They are the structure of love. They guide us in how to act in loving ways toward people, even when we may not feel particularly loving.

But there is still a problem. In chapter 3 we noted the chronic inability of people to keep God's commandments. It was the reason we needed to be rescued by Jesus. How does God's grace, revealed in Jesus, work a change in us? The answer is glimpsed in a surprising topic.

The Virgin Birth

For some, the idea of Jesus' virgin birth makes the Christian faith too ridiculous to believe. Of course if we believe the extraordinary idea that God became a human being in Jesus, then the virgin birth is a minor detail. In fact one wonders why God bothered with Mary at all. Why not simply appear as a human being without the gynecological complications?

The answer takes us back to the genealogy with which the New Testament begins. Matthew's gospel starts off with a list of Jesus' ancestors going back to Abraham. One purpose of this genealogy is to connect Jesus with the promises God made to Abraham, including the promise to give Abraham descendants through whom all the families of the earth would be blessed. But there is another purpose to this genealogy. It shows how unpromising was Jesus' ancestry.

The first person mentioned in the list is Abraham. When living in Egypt during a famine, Abraham tried to pass off his beautiful wife Sarah as his sister, so that Pharaoh, the king of Egypt, would not murder him in order to marry her (Genesis 12:10-20). In this case Abraham, the man of faith, shows a distressing lack of trust in God's promises.

In the next generation Abraham's son Isaac does the same thing with his wife Rebekah (Genesis 26:6-11). Then Judah, the fourth person in the list, impregnates his widowed daughter-in-law when she disguises herself as a prostitute (Genesis 38:1-30).

This genealogy is hardly a testimony to God's wise selection of a chosen people. Nor is it a promising family of origin for Jesus. To be sure, there are some noble figures in this genealogy, like Ruth and Hezekiah. But then there is David, who fathered Solomon after an affair with Bathsheba, whom he married after arranging to have her husband killed in combat.

This is Jesus' ancestry. Dig deep enough, and you will find similar stories in every family tree. The Bible does not say that sin is passed on through our genes, but it might as well be. As Paul says in Romans 5:12: "Therefore, just as sin came into the world through one man [Adam], and death came through sin, and so death spread to all because all have sinned..."

Jesus' family tree is no more encouraging than ours, except—and here is the twist—Jesus is not, strictly speaking, a descendant of this genealogy. The genealogy culminates in Joseph. But Jesus is not fathered by Joseph. Jesus is a work of the Holy Spirit in Mary, which means that Jesus is the beginning of a new creation.

The Christian belief in the virgin birth is not about gynecology. This is not like the stories of Greek mythology where the god Zeus impregnates a human female. Jesus, we are told, is conceived by the Holy Spirit, which means that in Jesus, God brings something new into the world.

Mary herself recognizes this. At first she is incredulous about the idea of giving birth as a virgin. But once she accepts that impossible possibility, she begins to see its larger implications. In a song traditionally called the *Magnificat* Mary says of God:

> He has shown strength with his arm; he has scattered the proud in the thoughts of their hearts. He has brought down the powerful from their thrones, and lifted up the lowly; he has filled the hungry with good things, and sent the rich away empty (Luke 1:51-53).

Isn't this a rather extreme way to talk about a pregnancy? Not when you consider the possibilities, implied by this pregnancy, of God doing something new and dramatic in the world.

The New Testament certainly claims that God became a human being in Jesus. That is part of what it means to say that Jesus was born of the Virgin Mary. But the virgin birth also means that Jesus is the beginning of a new possibility for human life. In Jesus our heredity no longer determines our destiny.

The apostle Paul expresses this in II Corinthians 5:17 when he says, "So if anyone is in Christ, there is a new creation; everything old has passed away; see everything has become new!" Jesus is not just another story in the sad history of human dysfunction passed on from generation to generation. He is the beginning of a new possibility for human life.

Fred Craddock tells the story of eating at a restaurant in the Great Smoky Mountains of Tennessee when he struck up a conversation with an elderly gentleman. The man asked what Craddock did for a living, and Craddock replied that he was a Christian minister. The man paused for a moment, then said, "I owe a great deal to a minister of the Christian church," and he pulled up a chair to sit down. Craddock wasn't sure he wanted the company, but he listened. The man said,

> My mother was not married, and the whole community knew it. I was what was called an illegitimate child. ...

> In my early teens I began to attend a little church back in the mountains. ... However, I was afraid that I was not welcome since I was, as they put it, a bastard. So I would go just in time for the sermon, and when it was over I would move out because I was afraid that someone would say "What's a boy like you doing in church?"

> One Sunday some people queued up in the aisle before I could get out, and I was stopped. Before I could make my way through the group, I felt a hand on my shoulder, a heavy hand. It was the minister. ... I knew what he was doing. He was going to make a guess as to who my father was. ... [But] he said, "Boy, you're a child of God. I see a striking resemblance." Then he swatted me on the bottom and said, "Now you go claim your inheritance." I left the building a different person.

Moved by the story, Craddock asked the man his name. The man said, "Ben Hooper," and Craddock realized he was talking to the twice-elected governor of Tennessee.[6]

In Jesus our heredity no longer determines our destiny. Our past no longer determines our future. God's grace opens up possibilities of transformation that can change our lives forever.

Grace, Predestination, and Free Will

Before we leave the discussion of grace and transformation, one other issue needs attention: the subject of predestination.

In Romans 8:28-29 the apostle Paul says,

We know that all things work together for good for those who love God, who are called according to his purpose. For those whom he foreknew he also predestined to be conformed to the image of his Son, in order that he might be the firstborn within a large family.

This is echoed in Ephesians 1:3-6:

Blessed be the God and Father of our Lord Jesus Christ, who has blessed us in Christ with every spiritual blessing in the heavenly places, just as he chose us in Christ before the foundation of the world to be holy and blameless before him in love. He destined us for adoption as his children through Jesus Christ, according to the good pleasure of his will, to the praise of his glorious grace that he freely bestowed on us in the Beloved.

These two scripture passages, especially the second, make the connection between grace and predestination. If a relationship with God is something that God gives us as a free act of grace, it must be something God chose for us, not something we chose for ourselves. This understanding of grace has been shared by Christian teachers throughout history, including the Apostle Paul, Saint Augustine, Martin Luther, John Calvin, and Karl Barth. Grace means that even our capacity to respond to God is itself a gift. We cannot take credit for our faith. It is a gift, for which the only proper response is gratitude.

The positive side of predestination is the humility it infuses in us. We cannot look down on people who believe differently than we do, as if our faith makes us morally superior. We can only share what faith has done for us and live with gratitude and compassion.

Predestination also provides a new perspective for viewing other people in the church. We may not have chosen some of the people who end up worshiping with us in church, but if they are there, then God chose them, and our job is to show them compassion and respect, even if we disagree with them at times about how to live as God's chosen people.

Of course predestination also raises problems, which for some may be a serious barrier to faith. If God causes everything that happens, then God is responsible for all the evil in the world. Predestination implies that God is all powerful but not all loving.

At the same time, predestination seems to strip human beings of free will, taking away the responsibility of those who choose not to believe in God, making any adverse consequences from this unjust. Even worse, it makes all of us—believers and non-believers—into robots incapable of a real relationship with God, which was the purpose for which we were created.

But the Bible never suggests that God's sovereignty over history nullifies human free will. Rather the Bible portrays God's will interacting with human decisions in an intricate dance. In the Bible, people make real decisions but God's ultimate purpose is still fulfilled.

Joseph, one of the twelve sons of Jacob, the great grandson of Abraham, was a spoiled brat. His father clearly favored him over the other children, to the point of giving Joseph a special robe and allowing him to stay at home while his brothers were out in the cold herding sheep. Even worse,

Jacob occasionally sent Joseph out to check on his brothers, and Joseph reported back unfavorable things about them, making their relationship even more strained. Then Joseph had the nerve to tell his brothers about a dream in which the bundles of wheat gathered by his brothers all bowed down to his bundle.

Finally, the brothers could stand it no longer. When Joseph showed up again to check on them, they seized him and sold him as a slave to a passing merchant headed for Egypt.

In Egypt, Joseph became the slave of an officer in Pharaoh's guard named Potiphar. No longer a pampered child, Joseph had to work hard. But he did a good job, and Potiphar promoted him. Unfortunately, Potiphar's wife also liked him. She tried to seduce him, and when he refused, she accused him of attempted rape. Joseph was thrown in prison for several years. In prison, however, he showed wisdom and kindness to the guards and other prisoners. He interpreted a dream for one of the prisoners, who was eventually released and restored to service in Pharaoh's palace.

Then one night Pharaoh had a dream. He dreamt that the cattle in his land became thin and died because of lack of food. He did not understand the dream, but his servant remembered how Joseph could interpret dreams. So Pharaoh sent for Joseph, and Joseph explained that a seven-year famine was coming during which crops would fail and people would starve. To prepare for it, Joseph organized the first government farm program: storing grain during the good years so there would be food to eat during the bad years. As a result, when the famine struck, everyone was forced to come to Egypt to get food, including Joseph's brothers. Without recognizing him, they bowed down to him, just as Joseph had foreseen in his dream.

This long, complicated story is a case study in predestination and free will. Was it God's will for Joseph to alienate his brothers? No. Was it God's will for the brothers to sell him into slavery? No. Was it God's will that Potiphar's wife would falsely accuse him of rape and that he would be unjustly imprisoned? No. All these things were done by people exercising their free will. Yet God used all these events for the ultimate purpose of saving Jacob and his family during a famine. Joseph points this out to his brothers at the end of the story: "Even though you intended to harm me, God intended it for good, in order to preserve a numerous people, as he is doing today" (Genesis 50:20).

In Romans 8 the apostle Paul says, "We know that all things work together for good for those who love God, who are called according to his purpose." Paul does not mean by this that God causes everything that happens. He means that God can work through anything that happens to fulfill God's purpose for us.

And that is the key to understanding Ephesians, chapter 1. Verses 9–10 tell us, "[God] has made known to us the mystery of his will, according to his good pleasure that he set forth in Christ, as a plan for the fullness of time, to gather up all things in him, things in heaven and things on earth."

Predestination means that God has a destiny for us in Christ. That destiny is reconciliation with God—bringing humans and the whole creation back into the relationship with God and with one another for which they were created. Within history, humans have free will and can try to thwart that destiny. But in the end they will not succeed. God is going to win. The question is whether we will be one of the barriers God must overcome to accomplish God's purpose, or whether we will be one of God's joyful instruments helping to bring it about.

Questions for Discussion

1. Reflect on your own family experience. Were feelings of love, acceptance, and perhaps even forgiveness something you earned by your actions? Or were they given freely apart from your actions? Or was it a combination of both? How did this affect you?

2. How do you feel about things like commandments and rules? When do you see them as helpful? Not helpful?

3. What are some characteristics or patterns you have inherited from your family? Which have been

helpful to you? Which have been things you had to overcome? What helped you with that?

4. Reflect on experiences of "providence" in your life—things that seemed to work out for a purpose of which you were unaware or only partially aware at the time. How did this work? What role did your actions play?

6

Where is the Kingdom?

One summer I served as a chaplain for a week of Boy Scout camp in northern Idaho. During lunch a Jewish scout asked me questions about what Christians believed and why there were so many different Christian denominations. At the end he said, "There's one thing I still don't understand. How can you Christians say that the Messiah has come when there is still so much suffering in the world?"

It is not just atheists like my debate partner Mike who see problems with the Christian faith. So have Jewish people going back to the time of Jesus. Luke tells us that one day the Pharisees came to Jesus asking when the kingdom of God would come (Luke 17:20). Prior to this Jesus had healed countless people, calmed a storm on the Sea of Galilee, and fed over 5000 people with five loaves of bread and two fish. But to the Pharisees the big question still remained: What about the problems of evil and injustice in the world? The Messiah is supposed to do something about that.

Philip Yancey tells of a Jewish friend who led tour groups of Christians visiting the Holy Land. As the friend listened to Christian groups talk about Jesus' second coming, it surprised him how similar it sounded to the Messiah he had learned about in Hebrew school: a righteous king bringing justice and peace to a fractured planet. He said to Philip Yancey, "Wouldn't it be amazing if we found out we were all waiting for the same person?"[1]

In a sense Christians and Jews are indeed waiting for the same person. We are waiting for the Messiah, God's chosen king, who will bring God's righteousness and peace to the world. The difference is that Christians are waiting for his *return*. The Messiah for whom we wait is none other than Jesus of Nazareth, who during his earthly life showed the depth of God's love for us on a cross and the power to make that love visible in earthly life.

But how can Jesus be the Messiah? A classic answer that I heard as a child goes something like this: Jesus is not an earthly king but a heavenly king. He came not to deal with the world's suffering but to take us out of the world into his heavenly kingdom where we will live eternally with him after we die.

Thanks to a youth leader in high school and some professors in college and seminary, I learned that this answer, though partly true, is not the whole story. The problem is the way it gives up on the created world. If the ultimate goal of the Christian life is to escape the world, what motive do we have for trying to make the world better? Does this not give Christians the reputation of being concerned only for ourselves?

Jesus, I learned, has a better answer.

Announcing the Kingdom

The Bible tells us that after Jesus' resurrection he appeared to his disciples for forty days speaking to them about the kingdom of God (Acts 1:3). This reiterates the way Jesus began his ministry. In his first recorded sermon Jesus says, "The time is fulfilled, and the kingdom of God has come near; repent and believe in the good news" (Mark 1:15). He repeats this theme throughout the gospels. During a synagogue service in his home town of Nazareth, Jesus reads these words of the prophet Isaiah: "The Spirit of the Lord is upon me, because he has anointed me to bring good news to the poor. He has sent me to proclaim release to the captives and recovery of sight to the blind, to let the oppressed go free, to proclaim the year of the Lord's favor" (Luke 4:18-19).

For the congregation in Nazareth, these words evoked a very earthly hope for their nation: that Israel would be set free from Roman oppression, that its political prisoners would be released, that the blind would be healed and the poor relieved of crushing debt, so that everyone could live in peace on their ancestral land.

Then in a startling comment Jesus says, "Today, this scripture has been fulfilled in your hearing." By this statement Jesus identifies himself as the "anointed one" of whom Isaiah speaks. In Hebrew the word for "anointed one" is *Messiah*; in Greek *Christ*. In thinly veiled language Jesus identifies himself as the Messiah or Christ who would inaugurate God's promised kingdom.

At various times in his ministry Jesus displays power to cast out demons. His opponents try to discredit him by saying he has this power because he is a demon-prince! But Jesus replies, "If Satan also is divided against himself, how will his kingdom stand? ... But if it is by the finger of God that I cast out demons, then the kingdom of God has come to you" (Luke 11:18, 20).

Everything Jesus did and said confirmed his identity as the "bringer of God's kingdom." At one point John the Baptist sends messengers asking Jesus, "Are you the one who is to come, or are we to wait for another?" Jesus replies, "Go and tell John what you have seen and heard: the blind receive their sight, the lame walk, the lepers are cleansed, the deaf hear, the dead are raised, and the poor have good news brought to them" (Luke 7:20-22).

Notice how Jesus' answer emphasizes the effect of his coming on earthly life. The disciples followed Jesus because they believed he was the one who would bring God's kingdom to this world. As noted in chapter 4, their faith was shattered when they saw Jesus die on a cross. But it revived and became stronger when they met him risen from the dead.

Now at the beginning of the book of Acts, after Jesus' resurrection, the disciples are wondering, "Lord, is this the time when you will restore the kingdom to Israel?" (Acts 1:6). In a way they are asking the same question as the Pharisees and the Jewish Boy Scout. Jesus, if you are the promised king, where is the kingdom?

The Hidden Presence of God's Kingdom

In Luke 17, according to the King James Version, Jesus answers the Pharisees with these words: "The kingdom of God cometh not with observation; neither shall they say, 'Lo here!' or 'Lo, there!' For behold the kingdom of God is within you" (Luke 17:20-21, KJV).

Some take this to mean that Jesus is not interested in a physical earthly kingdom, but in a spiritual kingdom established in our hearts.

In chapter 1, I made the point that Jesus came to make possible for us a personal relationship with God, the kind of relationship for which we were created. There is a sense in which the kingdom of God is present in Jesus, because a relationship to God is present in Jesus. The kingdom Jesus brings is, in part, a spiritual kingdom that begins in our hearts when we believe in him.

But that is not the whole story. When Jesus says, "The kingdom of God is within you," the Greek word translated "within" can also be translated "among." Hence in the New Revised Standard Version of Luke 17:21, Jesus says, "For, in fact, the kingdom of God is among you."

This gives a different feel to the meaning of God's kingdom. As I learned more about the Bible in college and seminary, I learned that the kingdom of God is not only a spiritual reality in our hearts. It is also a reality in human bodily existence where the hungry are fed, the sick are healed, the demons are cast out, the captives are freed, and the poor receive good news. When Jesus says that the kingdom of God is among you, he means it is present in his coming and given concrete form in his earthly ministry. But for now it is a partially hidden kingdom, not something to which you can point and say unequivocally that it has arrived.

To explain this Jesus tells a series of parables about the kingdom of God, all of which emphasize its hidden presence. He says,

> What is the kingdom of God like? And to what should I compare it? It is like a mustard seed that someone took and sowed in the garden; it grew and

became a tree, and the birds of the air made nests in its branches." And again he said, "To what should I compare the kingdom of God? It is like yeast that a woman took and mixed in with three measures of flour until all of it was leavened" (Luke 13:18-21).

Both of these parables describe the kingdom of God as something seemingly small and insignificant. A mustard seed when dropped on the ground virtually disappears. Nevertheless it is present in the ground, sending down roots, pushing up sprouts, and eventually becoming a plant in which birds can nest. Likewise when yeast is mixed into bread dough, you might not realize it is there. Nevertheless it is present in the dough, fermenting, bubbling, expanding, and eventually transforming the entire lump.

So it is with the kingdom of God. It is present in Jesus, but hidden. Its transforming power is not always apparent. But though unseen, it is there fermenting, bubbling, working a transformation in our lives that is not yet fully revealed.

A theologian name Oscar Cullman compared it to the relationship between D-day and V-day in World War II.[2] On D-day the allied troops established a beachhead on the coast of Normandy in France. It became the landing spot for thousands of tanks and other vehicles, not to mention hundreds of thousands of troops who poured into France and began the final assault against Hitler. One could argue that when the allied troops landed on Normandy the end of World War II was at hand. It did not happen right away, of course. It took months for the allies to work their way from Normandy to Berlin. There would be much more suffering and loss of life before V-day—the final Allied victory. But D-day was the turning point. On D-day liberation arrived in Europe, and it was only a matter of time before the victory was complete.

When Jesus came, God arrived on the beachhead of this world, and the power of sin and death was broken. Admittedly, the war is not over. We are still fighting our way across Europe. We are still battling the powers of sin and evil that destroy lives and relationships. But we know that we are going to win. With the arrival of Jesus the final victory is assured. Which means that if we continue to struggle, at least we struggle with hope and not despair.

Signs of the Kingdom

Though the arrival of God's kingdom was mostly hidden in the time of Jesus, and is still mostly hidden in our world today, nevertheless there are signs of it to be noticed.

In the gospel of John, Jesus' miracles are often referred to as "signs." After turning water into wine at the wedding in Cana, John says, "Jesus did this, the first of his signs, in Cana of Galilee, and revealed his glory, and his disciples believed in him" (John 2:11). Two chapters later, after Jesus heals the son of a royal official, John says, "Now this was the second sign that Jesus did after coming from Judea to Galilee" (John 4:54). In John chapter 6, Jesus feeds 5000 people with five loaves of bread and two fish, and John says, "When the people saw the sign that he had done, they began to say, 'This is indeed the prophet who is to come into the world'" (John 6:14).

Jesus performs an even greater sign by raising Lazarus from the dead. When Jesus enters Jerusalem to cheering crowds waving palm branches, John observes, "It was also because they heard that he had performed this sign [raising Lazarus] that the crowd went out to meet him" (John 12:18). Throughout John's gospel the coming of God's kingdom in Jesus is displayed through signs.

The enthusiasm of the crowd was dampened, however, when they realized that Jesus was not going to feed everyone who was hungry or cure everyone who was sick or raise everyone from the dead. The miracles Jesus did were preliminary signs of the kingdom. They were not the finished product. In Jesus a beachhead for the kingdom of God was established, but the final victory over all wrongdoing and suffering was still in the future.

In one of the churches I served, we had two members facing terminal cancer at the same time. Every week we prayed for both. Many additional prayers were offered by their family and friends. In one case the cancer inexplicably disappeared, causing the congregation to rejoice in God's miraculous healing. But a short time later the other person died, and we were left to wonder why one was healed and the other was not.

Some Christians argue that the difference is in the faith of the person desiring to be healed, or perhaps the faith of the one praying for healing. Christians with sufficient faith in God's power to heal will receive healing, while those lacking sufficient faith may not receive it.

To me this is not only untrue but detrimental. It contradicts the meaning of grace and adds unreasonable guilt to someone already suffering from illness. The better approach is to recognize that all healing in this life is temporary—a provisional sign of the ultimate healing yet to come.

This was true even during Jesus' earthly ministry. Every person whom Jesus healed eventually got sick again and died, even Lazarus. All healing in this life, even healing by Jesus, is provisional. The final healing will not take place until our resurrection.

So what does it mean when Jesus heals people? It means that Jesus is giving us a sign of the final healing yet to come. In reality God heals us all the time. Every day our bodies recover from illness and injury without us even thinking about it. But on occasion Jesus gives us unexpected healings as "signs." This sign does two things: 1) it reminds us of what God is doing all the time to heal our bodies, and 2) it gives us hope for what God will yet do in our lives, even after we die.

For me this understanding of healing has three important implications:

1. It avoids deism. Deism is the belief that God is like a watchmaker, creating the world and setting it running, but then leaving the world to its own devices, not interfering with the natural course of events. This leads to an impersonal God removed from our lives, the very opposite of the God portrayed in the Bible.
2. It avoids unwarranted guilt. It does not place blame for failed healing on the shoulders of the sick or those

praying for them, making them feel worse than they already do.

3. It offers hope. It suggests that whether healed or not we have a future—a purpose for our lives yet to be fulfilled.

Inviting Others to Share the Victory

In a 1993 movie called *Searching for Bobby Fisher*, a 7 year-old boy named Josh is taught to play chess by some street people in New York City. The boy has a natural talent for the game not seen since Bobby Fisher, the prodigy who won the United States Chess Championship as a teenager. The tension in the movie focuses on how hard the boy's coach will push to make him a champion and whether the boy will lose his compassionate heart in the process.

At the end of the movie Josh plays in the championship game of a tournament against another boy also driven by his coach to become the next Bobby Fisher. The parents and coaches are not allowed in the room where the game is played. They must watch on closed circuit television. Late in the game Josh's opponent makes a move, and Josh's coach in the other room says under his breath, "That was a mistake." Then, even though Josh cannot hear him, the coach begins talking as if he is talking to Josh. He says, "You've got him. It's there. Look deep, Josh. It's 12 moves away, but it's there. You've got him."

In the other room Josh is staring at the board. He senses he has been given an opening but he can't see it. Back in the coach's room the coach says under his breath, "Don't move until you see it." Josh stares at the board imagining every possible combination, until suddenly he looks up, and in his eyes you see that he has got it. He has seen the combination.

Then in the most remarkable scene of the movie, Josh reaches out to shake hands with his opponent. In the other room his father asks the coach, "What is he doing?" The coach says, "He's offering him a draw." Meanwhile in the game room Josh's opponent asks the same question: "What are you doing?" Josh says, "I'm offering you a draw. Take the draw, and we'll share the championship." His opponent says, "You've got to be kidding. Look at the board. I'm going to win." Josh says, "You've already lost, you just don't know it." But his opponent refuses the handshake, so Josh makes his move. In the process Josh loses a rook, but 11 moves later he wins.

I see in this movie a parable of Jesus and the kingdom of God. With the arrival of Jesus, the victory has been won. The forces of evil, oppression, greed, prejudice, violence, destruction, and death will not have the last word over us or over God's beloved creation. But many in the world do not yet know that. Like in the chess match, the victory is 12 moves away—an unknown number of lifetimes—which explains why many people cannot see it. It becomes even harder to see when Jesus' first move involves a sacrifice: his death on the cross. But the sacrifice assures the victory. Our job at this point is to offer our hand to others, even to our opponents, so they can share in that victory.

Why Are We Still Waiting?

Which brings me to one more question: why is it taking so long? Why are we still waiting for God's kingdom over 2000 years later?

After Jesus' resurrection, the disciples ask, "Lord, is this the time when you will restore the kingdom to Israel?" (Acts 1:6). The disciples' field of view is still limited to their own nation. In their minds, the kingdom is about what God will do for "us."

But Jesus replies, "It is not for you to know the times or periods that the Father has set by his own authority. But you will receive power when the Holy Spirit has come upon you; and you will be my witnesses in Jerusalem, in all Judea and Samaria, and to the ends of the earth" (Acts 1:7-8).

Jesus does not tell us when God's kingdom will come, but he gives us a job to do while we are waiting: to be witnesses to this coming kingdom and to the Lord who will reign over it.

Part of this job is to invite others to believe the good news of this coming kingdom and trust the Messiah who has inaugurated it. This allows us even now to share in the joy and hope of his triumph.

But another part of our job is giving glimpses to the world of how God's new kingdom will look. Hence we give food to people, or even better, empower people to feed themselves. We do this as a sign that in God's kingdom all God's children will have plenty to eat. We also work for justice and human rights as a sign that in God's kingdom the captives will be free. We provide health care to people who need it as a sign of the day when death will be no more, and we comfort the grieving as a sign of the day when God will wipe every tear from our eyes.

This is not to say that God's kingdom depends on our efforts. As I noted in chapter 3, the worst tyrants in history are those who thought they could create the kingdom of God through human means: the *Pax Romana* of Caesar, the Third Reich of Hitler, the proletariat of the people espoused by Marx and Lenin. As Lesslie Newbegin observed, "The project of bringing heaven down to earth always results in bringing hell up from below."[3]

But nor does this mean we should withdraw from the world and wait passively for its destruction. Jesus tells us to be witnesses, which means he invites us to be a sign of the kingdom, even as we wait for it.

This self-understanding not only gives us purpose, it saves us from despair. The problems of poverty and oppression are overwhelming, not only in the world but in our immediate communities. Nevertheless I join with others to address them, not because I think I can bring about the kingdom of God through charitable work or community organization, but because such actions testify to the nature of God's love for us. And because I believe in Jesus, I believe our efforts will not be in vain.

In 1984 during a civil war in Lebanon, a Presbyterian missionary named Benjamin Weir wrote an article for a mission publication explaining his work in that dangerous situation:

Our hopes focus on peace. The land of Lebanon has been marred, scarred, and charred with all the weapons of war imaginable to humankind. We are witnesses, here in Beirut, to homes destroyed and people brutalized in untold numbers. ... Our own efforts at rebuilding and renewing seem small and necessarily partial, but we are thankful that God has given us the opportunity to have a part in healing and rebuilding. We are part of the church's efforts to reestablish worship services, to assist persons moving back to villages, to encourage youth leadership, to give support to those whose hope lies in the future.

He then gave this moving appeal:

From our home to yours, we send this, our prayer for peace. The kingdom of God is a kingdom without weapons, without oppressive powers, without torture, without hunger—without exploitation of individuals and peoples, without prejudice, without an irresponsible use of what God has given us. It is a kingdom full of life, of faith, justice, peace, love— mutual understanding and reconciliation, of real possibilities for every human being. That is what we look toward, and we have no right as Christians to settle for anything less.[4]

That, to me, is a faith worth believing and worth living for. Yes, we believe in a Messiah whose kingdom has not yet fully come. But we have seen signs of that kingdom in Jesus' life, and the victory of that kingdom in his resurrection. So we serve him by our words and actions in the world, imperfect and limited as they are, inviting others to join us and share in the joyful reign of God that will not be thwarted and will never end.

Questions for Discussion

1. Where do you see in our world the most disturbing contradictions to the idea of a loving God? Where do

you see signs of a loving God at work in the world? How do you explain this discrepancy between a God who seems to be present and a God who seems to be absent?

2. When have you seen prayers for healing answered? When have you seen them not answered? How do you explain that difference?

3. What difference does Jesus' coming make in your own life? What difference does it make in the world? Is there a connection between these two things?

4. What do you see as your role in addressing the evils of the world? What makes you feel discouraged? What gives you hope?

7

The Flawed Representatives
of a New Creation

I grew up feeling at home and blessed by being part of a church. When I went to church with my grandparents, I sat with my grandfather while my grandmother sang in the choir. When I got restless during the sermon, he took me downstairs to the church boiler room where, miraculously, we found a small plate of cookies and two glasses of milk set out on a table. I never thought to wonder why there were cookies and milk in the boiler room; we just sat down, ate the cookies, drank the milk, and then went back upstairs just in time for the final hymn. I loved that church.

Everywhere we moved my parents sought out a church. As a 5 year-old I helped my father fold Sunday morning bulletins run on a mimeograph machine. Later I helped my mother assemble materials for her Vacation Bible School class. In every church they attended, they made friends who knew me by name and asked about what I was doing in school or sports.

When I was in Junior High, my father retired from the Air Force and we settled down in Lakewood, Washington, where I joined the confirmation class of a Presbyterian Church. As a high school student, I became a teacher in the children's ministry of the church and later a counselor at a church camp.

In my senior year of high school I was elected as a youth representative to the national General Assembly of the

Presbyterian Church. It was my first real taste of the church's worldwide mission. An amazing array of delegates from all over the world told of how God was working in their countries.

This led me in college to become a candidate for ministry in the Presbyterian Church, and after college I attended seminary in Princeton, New Jersey. There I met scholars who opened my eyes to the meaning of Bible stories in a way I had never before experienced. They showed me a God who wanted not only to change our hearts but to change the world—that in fact changing the world and changing our hearts went together.

Eventually, I became a minister of the gospel and served three wonderful churches over 39 years: a Lutheran-Presbyterian shared ministry in Potlatch, Idaho, and then Presbyterian Churches in Spokane and Des Moines, Washington. These churches were not without issues and conflicts, but in each of them I was impressed with how much people cared about each other and at least tried to be nice to each other, even when disagreeing, which is more than I can say for many other institutions in our society.

So I have had wonderful experiences in churches all my life, and I have always had a deep and abiding appreciation for this much maligned institution. But I also recognize that for many people their experience of church has not been so pleasant.

The Problem of the Church

In a magazine called *Presbyterian Survey*, I saw a cartoon depicting two people sitting under a tree. The first says, "Power struggles, mistrust, divisive issues, economic woes. Sigh! Sometimes it gets to be too much." The other says, "Good thing we have the church, huh?" The first says, "I was talking about the church."[1]

Recently I read a book by David Kinnamon and Gabe Lyons called *UnChristian: What a New Generation Really Thinks about Christianity*. It was based on a national survey of young adults who don't go to any church and don't want to. They are what the book calls "young outsiders." The authors write,

> In our national surveys we found the three most common perceptions of present day Christianity [by young outsiders] are anti-homosexual (an image held by 91% of young outsiders), judgmental (87%), and hypocritical (85%). These "big three" are followed by the following negative perceptions, embraced by a majority of young adults: old-fashioned, too involved in politics, out of touch with reality, insensitive to others, [and] boring."[2]

Ouch. For many people, Christians in general and the church in particular give them reasons not to believe in Christianity. This is aggravated by the horrifying experiences of people being abused by church leaders, or demeaned and discriminated against in churches.

In a book called *God Is Not Great: How Religion Poisons Everything*, Christopher Hitchens tells this story:

> In Belfast, I have seen whole streets burned out by sectarian warfare between different sects of Christianity, and interviewed people whose relatives and friends have been kidnapped and killed or tortured by rival religious death squads, often for no other reason than membership of another confession. There is an old Belfast joke about the man stopped at a roadblock and asked his religion. When he replies that he is an atheist he is asked, "Protestant or Catholic atheist?"[3]

I find this an interesting example. When a person in Belfast can be asked about being a Protestant or Catholic atheist, the issue is obviously not the person's belief. It's the person's affiliation. It was not a belief in God or even a belief in Jesus that caused the problems in Northern Ireland. Both sides believed in God and Jesus. It was the actions of people calling themselves Protestants or Catholics. Hitchens' example does not indict the faith of Christianity as much as particular communities of believers whom we call the church.

In the first congregation I served as a pastor, one of the elders tried to invite a neighbor to our church. The neighbor said, "I don't want to go to that church. It is full of hypocrites." The elder replied, "That's okay. There is always room for one more."

To say that Christian churches are full of hypocrites is to affirm one of Christianity's central tenets: that all of us are sinners in need of God's grace, not just at one time in our lives but continually. It should come as no surprise, then, that the church is an embarrassment to its own faith. The Christian faith predicts this.

In the gospel of Matthew, Jesus tells a parable about wheat and weeds.

> The kingdom of heaven may be compared to someone who sowed good seed in his field; but while everybody was asleep, an enemy came and sowed weeds among the wheat, and then went away. So when the plants came up and bore grain, then the weeds appeared as well (Matthew 13:24-26).

The church has always been a mixed bag. As the parable continues, the servants of the landowner offer to go through the field and pull out all the weeds, but the landowner says, "No; for in gatherings the weeds you would uproot the wheat along with them" (Matthew 13:29).

Back in chapter 3, I shared Aleksandr Solzhenitsyn's insight that the line dividing good and evil cuts through the heart of every human being. The church is filled with flawed human beings, just like every other institution. When we remember the story on which the church is based—the story of a Savior who died for our sins on a cross—this should not surprise us. The surprise is what draws these dysfunctional people together: the belief that God, through Jesus, will yet save us and our world from the consequences of our stupidity. In an ironic way the flaws of the church make plain the wondrous grace of the gospel: that we live not by our goodness but by God's grace, and that God's grace can do more good even in flawed people like us than we ever imagined.

But that still raises a question: Shouldn't the Christian church be, if not perfect, at least better than other human institutions? Why does it sometimes seem worse?

C. S. Lewis was once asked, "If Christianity is true, why are not all Christians obviously nicer than non-Christians?" Here is part of his response:

> Christian Miss Bates may have an unkinder tongue than unbelieving Dick Firkin. That, by itself, does not tell us whether Christianity works. The question is what Miss Bates' tongue would be like if she were not a Christian and what Dick's would be like if he became one. Miss Bates and Dick, as a result of natural causes and early upbringing, have certain temperaments: Christianity professes to put both temperaments under new management if they will allow it to do so.[4]

The glory of the church is not its perfection but its hope: that the God who began a good work in us will one day bring it to completion through Jesus Christ (Philippians 1:6).

A Community Containing the Seeds of Its Reform

There is no denying that throughout history Christian churches have committed atrocities, often justifying them in the name of Jesus. And yet their very claim to follow Jesus lays them open to the reforming power of his story.

At a pastoral conference I attended, William Willimon told about his first pastoral assignment at a small church in South Carolina. The year was 1968, and the town was in the middle of a major controversy over school desegregation. At the peak of the controversy there was a town meeting. Speaker after speaker stood up to denounce the whole idea of school integration, warning about what would happen if "they" were allowed to attend "our" schools. This went on for some time, mostly in angry tirades, until finally an old Southern Baptist minister raised his hand. He had been a pastor in the community for over 30 years. He had baptized, married, or buried almost everyone in town, or at least one of their relatives. When he raised his hand, a hush fell over the meeting. Slowly he made his way to the front and looked over the crowd. Then he began reading from the Bible— Galatians 3:28: "There is no longer Jew or Greek, there is no longer slave or free, there is no longer male and female; for all of you are one in Christ Jesus." He closed the book and said, "Go home and read your Bibles," and he sat down. After that, Willimon said, the meeting lost some of its steam. People began drifting away. Two weeks later the schools in that community desegregated without incident.

The church may be a flawed institution, but it is created by a story with the power to challenge its actions. Admittedly, this does not happen as fast or as often as one would hope. It took centuries for the vast majority of Christian churches to reject slavery, and many are still working on the lingering effects of racial discrimination. But there is hope, because the church acknowledges its accountability to Someone greater than itself. That Someone has been revealed in the story of Jesus, a story that continually undermines our pride and animosity, if we read it faithfully.

The Transforming Power of Community

Given the negative view of the church by many people today, one wonders why it grew so dramatically during its first three centuries. According to the book of Acts, there were approximately 120 followers of Jesus in the early days after his resurrection (Acts 1:15). By 300 A. D., even by conservative estimates, there were about 6 million Christians, enough that the Emperor Constantine thought it advantageous to become one. It is important to note that Christianity did not grow dramatically only after Constantine's conversion. Rather Constantine converted because by his time Christianity already had a significant presence in the Roman Empire.[5] How did that happen?

Sociologist Rodney Stark has investigated this question, and one of the factors he identifies is the transforming power of the early Christian community. He writes,

> In this book's closing chapters I will examine how Christianity served as a revitalization movement that arose in response to the misery, chaos, fear, and brutality of life in the urban Greco-Roman world. In anticipation of those discussions, let me merely suggest here that Christianity revitalized life in Greco-Roman cities by providing new norms and new kinds of social relationships able to cope with many urgent urban problems. To cities filled with the homeless and impoverished, Christianity offered charity as well as hope. To cities filled with newcomers and strangers, Christianity offered an immediate basis for attachments. To cities filled with orphans and widows, Christianity provided a new and expanded sense of family. To cities torn by violent ethnic strife, Christianity offered a new basis for solidarity. And to cities faced with epidemics, fires, and earthquakes, Christianity offered effective nursing services.[6]

Stark is not arguing as a philosopher or theologian for the truth of Christianity's claims. He is arguing as a sociologist for the power of Christian community.

In many ways the very process of being a community called together by Jesus forces us to grow out of ourselves. C. S. Lewis said that when he first became a Christian he did not like going to church, but he went because he thought he was supposed to. But as he went something began to happen in him. He writes,

> I disliked very much their hymns, which I considered to be fifth-rate poems set to sixth-rate music. But as I went on I saw the great merit of it. I came up against different people of quite different outlooks and different education, and then gradually my conceit began peeling off. I realized that the hymns (which

were just sixth-rate music) were, nevertheless, being sung with devotion and benefit by an old saint in elastic-side boots in the opposite pew, and then you realize that you aren't fit to clean those boots. It gets you out of your solitary conceit.[7]

I don't agree with Lewis' evaluation of church music, but I share his experience of how being part of a church helps us grow as followers of Christ.

I remember visiting a new attender at the church I served in Spokane, Washington. I asked the person what he was looking for in a church. He said, "I just want a church where everyone thinks the way I do."

Sometimes the church is helpful to us because it is not a place where everyone thinks the way we do. I have never been part of a church where everyone supported the same political party or liked the same Christian music or shared the same views about same-sex marriage. Becoming part of a church is like getting married. You may love your spouse, in this case Jesus, but the rest of the family comes with the package.

It was that way even for Jesus' first followers. Among the first twelve disciples were a tax collector, working as a collaborator for the Romans, and a zealot committed to the violent overthrow of the Romans. Even when the differences were not that drastic, there were still conflicts. When James and John asked to be given special places in Jesus' kingdom, the other disciples were enraged. Jesus called them together and said,

> You know that among the Gentiles those whom they recognize as their rulers lord it over them, and their great ones are tyrants over them. But it is not so among you; but whoever wishes to become great among you must be your servant, and whoever wishes to be first among you must be slave of all. For the Son of Man came not to be served but to serve, and to give his life a ransom for many (Mark 10:42-45).

The very story that draws us together forces us to treat each other differently than we might have on our own. And God uses that process to work on us, shaping us into the people God meant us to be.

In one of the churches I served as pastor, there was a man named Bo. Bo was the kind of person who rubbed me the wrong way. He frequently talked about himself, recounting how successful he was in business and how much money he had made. He ranted about how bad the government was and criticized what he called the lazy good-for-nothing people on welfare. He had opinions about everything, including our church, of which he was not even officially a member.

But then our church got involved with a program called Project Home Again. In the past our church had sponsored a refugee family from Southeast Asia, helping them resettle in the United States. Project Home Again was an attempt to do the same thing with a homeless family already living in our community.

When we took on this project, we invited people in the church to attend a meeting about it, and Bo showed up. Not only did he show up, but because he was a take-charge kind of person, he ended up as the chairman of the project.

I wasn't sure how this would turn out, but the result shocked me. Bo led the charge to help this family find a good apartment and personally paid their first two months' rent. He put out a call in the church for furniture and arranged for one of the church members with a truck to pick it up and haul it to their apartment. Then he helped the parents get their children enrolled in the public school and led the drive to get them school supplies. He helped the parents look for jobs and organized people in the church to provide transportation. Then, when it became apparent that the father could not work because of a back injury, Bo helped the father apply for and get Social Security disability. This man who could not stand government welfare helped this homeless father get on disability! And when the father's first disability check came, the father gave 10% of it to our church in the form of a check which Bo proudly brought into my office.

At least three transformations took place in this experience. First was the transformation that took place in the family. They went from being receivers to givers, including giving to God. Second was the transformation of Bo. I would have never imagined Bo in this role, but of course the very characteristics of Bo that bugged me, like his grandiose habit of taking charge, made him a force to be reckoned with in helping this family. And finally, there was the transformation in me. I learned not to pre-judge what God can or cannot do in the lives of people I may not like, and in the process I gained a friend. None of these transformations would have been possible without the flawed collection of people known as the church.

The Power of Sacraments

This is perhaps a good point to mention the role of baptism and communion in the Christian faith. All Christian churches baptize and share the Lord's Supper, but not all practice these sacraments in the same way. Some churches baptize infants; others only people old enough to make a decision to be baptized. Some immerse the whole person in water; others sprinkle water on the head. Some churches serve communion at the front; others pass the trays of bread and wine (or grape juice) to the people where they are seated. Some churches regard these elements to be symbolic of Jesus' body and blood; others regard them as in some way transformed into the real body and blood of Christ when consecrated in the church service. But all Christian churches regard these acts as 1) joining us into a relationship with Jesus, and 2) joining us into a relationship with each other.

First baptism. The apostle Paul says, "But now that faith has come, we are no longer subject to a disciplinarian, for in Christ Jesus you are all children of God through faith. As many of you as were baptized into Christ have clothed yourselves with Christ" (Galatians 3:25-27).

To use a more contemporary image, before Jesus we were like foster children, but in baptism we are adopted into Jesus' family. Can a person be a child of God without baptism? Of course. But baptism, in a sense, solidifies our relationship to God, somewhat like the difference between being a foster child and an adopted child. It identifies us in a tangible way as belonging to God, much as circumcision did for the people of Israel in the Old Testament, only baptism can be received by both men and women.

At the same time, however, baptism joins us to each other in the family of faith, just as adoption joins a child not only to the parents but to the siblings in the family. Hence Paul continues the scripture just quoted by saying, "There is no longer Jew or Greek, there is no longer slave or free, there is no longer male and female; for all of you are one in Christ Jesus" (Galatians 3:28).

Communion functions in a similar way. While baptism is generally a one-time event, like adoption, communion is a repeated event, more like Sunday dinner. A family dinner shared together is not just about eating, it is about reinforcing the ties to the family. Referring to communion, the apostle Paul says, "The cup of sharing that we bless, is it not a sharing in the blood of Christ? The bread that we break, is it not a sharing in the body of Christ?" (I Corinthians 10:16). However we understand it, communion is meant to reinforce our connection to Jesus. But at the same time communion joins us to each other in Jesus' family. Paul goes on to say, "Because there is one bread, we who are many are one body, for we all partake of the one bread" (I Corinthians 10:17). Communion, in other words, is necessarily communal. To become a follower of Jesus includes becoming part of his "body" in the world, called the church.

Serving in Ways We Could Not Do Alone

The church allows us to be witnesses to God's kingdom in ways we could not do alone. We saw that dramatically with Project Home Again. Bo did not help that homeless family by himself. Others in the church brought furniture and food, provided transportation and job contacts, visited the family and made them feel welcome in our church. It worked because the people of the church networked together to meet the need.

As a child, when I did not finish my dinner, I was told to remember the starving children in Africa. At that point I would have gladly given them my dinner, but that was impossible, or so I thought.

Then I went to college, and our student association arranged with the dining hall for a 24-hour fast by any interested students. The students agreed to skip all meals that day, and the dining hall agreed to use the money saved to help an international Christian relief organization feed hungry people in other parts of the world.

I learned from this an important concept: through worldwide church partnerships I can take money I might have used for something else and give it to starving, homeless, or displaced people in many parts of the world. Of course churches are not the only means of doing that. But it illustrates how churches enable us to work together, responding to needs that none of us could handle alone. Alone I cannot build a home for a homeless family, but through Habitat for Humanity I helped build one. Alone I cannot give an education to a poor child in Ecuador, but through Compassion International I helped do that. Alone I cannot train a new generation of pastors in Cuba, but through the Presbyterian Church mission agency I helped do that. All this is possible because Christians work together in worldwide communities of faith.

The task Jesus gave us to be witnesses to his coming kingdom forces us to depend on one another. The apostle Paul told the first century Christians in Corinth,

> For just as the body is one and has many members, and all the members of the body, though many, are one body, so it is with Christ. For in the one Spirit we were all baptized into one body—Jews or Greeks, slaves or free—and we were all made to drink of one Spirit. Indeed, the body does not consist of one member but of many. If the foot would say, "Because I am not a hand, I do not belong to the body," that would not make it any less a part of the body. And if the ear would say, "Because I am not an eye, I do

not belong to the body," that would not make it any less a part of the body. If the whole body were an eye, where would the hearing be? If the whole body were hearing, where would the sense of smell be? (I Corinthians 12:12-17).

Paul writes these words to a congregation riddled with divisions and hypocrisy. (Read the whole of I Corinthians for more details.) But Paul pleads with these divided Christians to see how crucial they are to one another for their mission as servants of Christ. When we serve Jesus together as part of a church, we associate with other flawed Christians to do things that none of us could do alone. Yes, we are hypocrites in the sense that our lives never measure up to Jesus' message of love. But, fortunately, there is always room for one more.

Prayer and Community

Every church I have known shares prayer concerns with others in the church family. They may do this through an email prayer chain, through written prayer requests, or through prayer requests voiced in church services. But all churches believe in lending our voices, or at least our thoughts, to the prayer concerns of others.

Why do we do this? It is not because we think God is ignorant of our concerns until we voice them. Nor do we think a critical mass of people must pray about something before God listens, as if God were a government official needing to be lobbied. So why do we feel this need to pray together?

In chapter 1, I mentioned that prayer is a way of building a personal relationship to God. The very act of praying, even when we say things that God already knows, fulfills part of the purpose for which we were created.

But there is another dimension to prayer. Pascal is widely quoted as saying, "God instituted prayer to communicate to creatures the dignity of causality."[8]

If you wonder why we should pray, you might also wonder why we should do anything. God can certainly put food on the table or clothes on our backs without our help. Jesus said, "Look at the birds of the air; they neither sow nor reap nor gather into barns, and yet your heavenly Father feeds them" (Matthew 6:26). God does not need our help to feed and clothe our families. So why should we work?

We work because through work God gives us the dignity of causality—the honor of actually participating in God's work. And the same applies to prayer.

A statement widely attributed to Karl Barth says, "To clasp the hands in prayer is the beginning of an uprising against the disorder of the world."[9] In this sense prayer is a form of witness. When not used for trivial convenience, it is a crucial part of our service to God in the world. God dignifies our prayers by allowing them to make a difference, and God magnifies that difference when we pray together.

This explains why Jesus said to his disciples, "Again, truly I tell you, if two of you agree on earth about anything to ask, it will be done for you by my Father in heaven. For where two or three are gathered in my name, I am there among them" (Matthew 18:19-20). Jesus does not mean that God requires a quorum before hearing our pleas for help. Rather God wants us to learn the value of praying, worshiping, and working together, because in doing so we serve God in a more profound way than any of us could alone.

A Life Not in Vain

We do not build the kingdom of God; it is a gift of God's grace. But the graciousness of that gift includes the way God uses us in its formation. We are witnesses to God's work, but in a sense we are also contributors.

In his first letter to the Corinthians, the apostle Paul describes how his own work as an apostle combines with the grace of God and the work of others to produce something unexpectedly precious. He writes,

> According to the grace of God given to me, like a skilled master builder I laid a foundation, and someone else is building on it. Each builder must choose with care how to build on it. For no one can lay any foundation other than the one that has been laid; that foundation is Jesus Christ (I Corinthians 3:10-11).

This seemingly contradictory statement captures the dynamic of grace and works, faith and witness. Jesus has laid the foundation for God's new creation. But Paul is graciously allowed to participate by building on it. He is given the dignity of causality. And so are we. When we feed the hungry, house the homeless, comfort the grieving, confront injustice, and invite others into a personal relationship with God, we not only give an example of how God's coming kingdom will look, we help shape it. Our partial, imperfect actions get built into its structure.

The book of Revelation captures this in its picture of the New Jerusalem coming down from heaven at the end of time with twelve foundations named after the twelve apostles (Revelation 21:14). The Bible is clear that the New Jerusalem is a gift. It comes down from heaven. Jesus is its cornerstone. And yet the lives and testimony of his followers are built into its structure.

Describing his own call to ministry through a vision of the risen Christ, the apostle Paul says,

> Last of all, as to one untimely born, he appeared also to me. For I am the least of the apostles, unfit to be called an apostle, because I persecuted the church of God. But by the grace of God I am what I am, and his grace toward me was not in vain. On the contrary, I worked harder than any of them—though it was not I, but the grace of God that is with me (I Corinthians 15:8-10).

Paul would not think for a moment that his work earned his acceptance by God. But through the grace of God his work made a difference. The grace of God did not nullify his work; it incorporated it.

In the rest of I Corinthians 15, Paul describes how our future resurrection from the dead is made possible by Jesus' resurrection. He concludes by saying, "Therefore, my beloved, be steadfast, immovable, always excelling in the work of the Lord, because you know that in the Lord your labor is not in vain" (I Corinthians 15:58).

This understanding of faith gives my life meaning and hope. If I really thought that everything depended on me, I would feel the constant pressure of responsibility, the pressure to do everything I could to make the world right, or at least to set right the lives of people around me. I would become a nervous wreck, and probably insufferable. But if I thought that nothing I did mattered, that my feeble life was irrelevant to the problems of the world or the people I cared about, then I would feel depressed. The knowledge that God's kingdom is in God's hands gives me hope, and the knowledge that what I do to serve Jesus can actually make a difference gives my life meaning.

Stewardship of Creation

This brings me to the Christian doctrine of stewardship. We are not the owners of God's creation, free to do with it whatever we want. We are stewards of that creation, set apart by God to be its caretakers for the good of all. This, I believe, expresses what God meant in Genesis 1 by giving humans "dominion" over the creation. The same idea is expressed in Genesis 2, verse 15: "Then the Lord God took the man and put him in the garden of Eden to till it and keep it." As the chapter goes on to explain, the woman was created to be a partner in this process. God made us responsible for the creation, charged with the mission to make the whole creation the blessing that God meant it to be.

Nietzsche was wrong to suggest that we must choose between caring about this life and sacrificing ourselves for a future one. The Bible suggests that the two go together. We prepare for the new creation by being faithful caretakers of this one. We prepare for God's kingdom by being compassionate and caring citizens of our earthly kingdoms, knowing that no earthly kingdom is absolute and that all will be judged by God.

Which brings me in the next chapter to a second look at the problem of evil.

Questions for Discussion

1. Reflect on your past experiences in a church or around church people. What in those experiences was a blessing to you? What was frustrating or off-putting?

2. How might the teachings or actions of Jesus reform the church today? What would Jesus want changed? What would Jesus want to encourage?

3. When have you been part of a group of people accomplishing something together that you never could have done on your own? How did your gifts fit in with others to help make that happen?

4. What does it mean for you to be a "caretaker of the garden"—a steward of God's creation?

8

Revisiting the Problem of Evil

My debate partner Mike offered three alternatives to the problem of evil:

1. God exists but is not all powerful
2. God exists but is not all loving
3. There is no God, only impersonal forces of nature

But there is a fourth alternative: that God exists and is not yet finished with the world.

A God Not Yet Finished

A man stopped on his way home from work to watch his son's Little League baseball game. When he got to the game, he asked one of the boys "What's the score?" The boy said cheerfully, "We're behind 14-0." The father said, "You don't sound very discouraged." The boy replied, "Why should I be? We haven't gotten up yet."

For Christians the answer to the problem of evil is that God still has another at bat. Our hope for this was established by Jesus' resurrection.

As a child, Easter gave me hope that my family and I would be reunited after we died. This is still for me an important meaning of Easter. But thanks to a seminary professor, I came to realize that Jesus' resurrection was more than that. It was a down payment on God's promise to redeem creation and bring blessing to the world. It demonstrated that injustice and suffering would not have the last word in our lives. Coming on the first day of the week, it symbolically represented the beginning of a new creation.

Revelation 21 brings the Bible story to a climax with these words:

> Then I saw a new heaven and a new earth; for the first heaven and the first earth had passed away, and the sea was no more. And I saw the holy city, the new Jerusalem, coming down out of heaven from God, prepared as a bride adorned for her husband. And I heard a loud voice from the throne saying, "See, the home of God is among mortals. He will dwell with them; they will be his peoples, and God himself will be with them; he will wipe every tear from their eyes. Death will be no more; mourning and crying and pain will be no more, for the first things have passed away" (Revelation 21:1-4).

Jesus resurrection anticipates and gives assurance of this final victory. If Jesus had not been raised, then the forces of evil in the world would not have been defeated; they would have been victorious. Pilate would have won! Once again history would have demonstrated that might makes right. But Jesus' resurrection changes that equation. Jesus' resurrection means that God triumphs over the power of murderous dictators and travesties of justice. Admittedly, there is still plenty of oppression and injustice in the world, but having seen what God can do in Jesus' life, we look forward to what God will yet do in the world, bringing God's justice and peace to all people.

Meanwhile, because of Jesus' resurrection we have a new identity and a mission to go with it. The apostle Paul tells the Corinthians,

> So if anyone is in Christ, there is a new creation: everything old has passed away; see, everything has become new! All this is from God, who reconciled us to himself through Christ, and has given us the ministry of reconciliation; that is, in Christ God was

reconciling the world to himself, not counting their trespasses against them, and entrusting the message of reconciliation to us. So we are ambassadors for Christ, since God is making his appeal through us; we entreat you on behalf of Christ, be reconciled to God (II Corinthians 5:17-20).

Not only does God promise a new creation when Jesus returns, but God is already beginning to make us part of it. Even now we are ambassadors of God's new creation.

At present this work in us is unfinished. We see it only in bits and pieces, with numerous relapses and setbacks. But in spite of our ongoing struggle with sin, we are representatives of Jesus' new kingdom, even as we wait for it. And that kingdom will one day embody God's victory over all sin and death in the world, including everything that alienates us from God and from one another.

In his discussion of Jesus' resurrection Paul concludes with these words:

Death has been swallowed up in victory. Where, O death is your victory? Where, O death is your sting? The sting of death is sin, and the power of sin is the law. But thanks be to God who gives us the victory through our Lord Jesus Christ. Therefore, my beloved, be steadfast, immovable, always excelling in the work of the Lord, because you know that in the Lord your labor is not in vain (I Corinthians 15:54-58).

Notice how Paul describes Jesus' resurrection as more than a victory over death. It is also a victory over sin, and over the evil and suffering that sin has brought into the world. Admittedly that victory is not yet complete, but a decisive battle has been won. Which means that our work to serve Jesus in this life—our battles against suffering, hunger, disease, injustice, and everything else that conspires to destroy lives and relationships—will not be in vain. Rather it will be fulfilled in the new heaven and earth brought into being by our risen Lord.

The Corollary of Resurrection: Understanding God's Judgment

A woman in my congregation asked to speak with me after a sermon I did on the resurrection. She was distraught. Even at a young age, she had experienced a rough life, including abuse at the hands of her husband. But the idea of the resurrection gave her no comfort. She said to me, "I don't want to go to heaven if my ex-husband will be there."

The kingdom of God will not be a realm of righteousness, peace, and joy, unless it is accompanied by God's judgment against the forces of injustice, hate, prejudice, and violence.

In a book called *Love Wins*, Rob Bell reflects on this. He begins with a review of the Old Testament prophets, who in their own time could be preachers of hell-fire and brimstone.

> Central to their vision of human flourishing in God's renewed world, then, was the prophets' announcement that a number of things that can survive in this world will not be able to survive in the world to come. Like war. Rape. Greed. Injustice. Violence. Pride. Division. Exploitation. Disgrace.

He continues,

> It is important to remember this the next time we hear people say they can't believe in a "God of judgment." Yes, they can. Often, we can think of little else. Every oil spill, every report of another woman sexually assaulted, every news report that another political leader has silenced the opposition through torture, imprisonment, and execution, every time we see someone stepped on by an institution or corporation more interested in profit than people, every time we stumble upon one more instance of the human heart gone wrong, we shake our fist and cry out, "Will somebody please do something about this?"[1]

Of course God's judgment does not fall only on institutions and political leaders; it falls on all of us. In the previous chapter I mentioned Paul's description of building on the foundation of Christ (I Corinthians 3). But as he talks about that image, he finds himself reflecting not only on God's grace but on God's judgment.

> Now if anyone builds on the foundation with gold, silver, precious stones, wood, hay, straw—the work of each builder will become visible, for the Day will disclose it, because it will be revealed with fire, and the fire will test what sort of work each has done. If what has been built on the foundation survives, the builder will receive a reward. If the work is burned up, the builder will suffer loss; the builder will be saved, but only as through fire (I Corinthians 3: 12-15).

Commenting on this, Lesslie Newbegin writes,

> Following that way [the path of Jesus], we can commit ourselves without reserve to all the secular work our shared humanity requires of us, knowing that nothing we do in itself is good enough to form part of that city's building, knowing that everything—from our most secret prayers to our most public acts—is part of that sin-stained human nature that must go down into the valley of death and judgment, and yet knowing that as we offer it up to the Father in the name of Christ and in the power of the Spirit, it is safe with him, and—purged in fire—it will find its place in the holy city at the end.[2]

Three things here deserve special comment:

1. Even Christians—perhaps especially Christians—have things in their lives that need to be judged, that need to be "burned up" by God in order to be ready for God's kingdom.
2. There is a difference between God's judgment of us as persons and God's judgment of what we have done.

We are saved by grace, not by works, which means we can be saved and brought into God's kingdom even if our works do not measure up.

3. And yet, even with salvation by grace there is still a "reward" for our works. The reward is in seeing how the things we do contribute to God's kingdom instead of being wasted.

Which brings me to the meaning of hell.

The Garbage Pit

In the gospels the word "hell" is a translation of the Greek word *Gehenna*, which means literally "valley of Hinnom"—an actual valley just outside the walls of Jerusalem. How did this valley come to be associated with hell?

The valley of Hinnom is mentioned several times in the Old Testament, always in connection with horrific acts of idolatry. II Chronicles 28:3 says that King Ahaz "made offerings in the valley of the son of Hinnom, and made his sons pass through fire, according to the abominable practices of the nations whom the Lord drove out before the people of Israel." In other words, the valley of Hinnom was a place where children were offered as sacrifices to gods other than the Lord. This is confirmed by the prophet Jeremiah when he condemns the people of Judah saying, "And they go on building the high place of Topheth, which is in the valley of the son of Hinnom, to burn their sons and their daughters in the fire—which I did not command, nor did it come into my mind" (Jeremiah 7:31).

By the time of Jesus, the valley of Hinnom—Gehenna in Greek—had such bad associations, it became the Jerusalem garbage dump, a first century landfill smoldering from the burning gases produced by rotting garbage.[3] Which explains why Jesus describes Gehenna with these words: "where the worm never dies and the fire is never quenched" (Mark 9:48). In the end those who practice hate and destruction end up on the trash heap of history. Hell—Gehenna—is the image Jesus uses for lives that are wasted.

But the things we do to serve Jesus will not be wasted in the resurrection; they will be fulfilled. Jesus reminds us that the kingdom of God is like a mustard seed. When you plant it, you may not at first see any discernable result. But that seed carries within it the power to be a great bush. Likewise, the things we do for God's kingdom, even if small and unnoticed, have the power to grow into something greater than we ever imagined. They are built into the fabric of the new heaven and earth where people will give thanks for them forever.

The Defeat of Satan

One of the first things to be eradicated in the kingdom of God is Satan.

Satan is, perhaps, the most misunderstood figure in the Bible. The word *satan* comes from a Hebrew word that means "adversary" or "accuser." Sometimes it refers to a military or political adversary (I Samuel 29:4, II Samuel 19:22, I Kings 11:14, 23, 25). But often it refers to an adversary in a legal case—an accuser. For example, Psalm 109 expresses the consternation of a person unfairly charged with wrongdoing. In verse 6 the person recites the words of those conspiring against him: "They say, 'Appoint a wicked man against him; let an accuser [*satan*] stand on his right. When he is tried, let him be found guilty; let his prayer be counted as sin.'"

The Greek word for adversary or accuser is *diabolos*, from which we get the word "devil." Both *satan* and *diabolos* conjure up the image of an adversary in a trial who accuses us and tries to get us convicted and punished. Satan, in other words, is like a prosecutor.

This is critical to understanding the three places in the Old Testament where the word Satan is used as a proper noun. One is the famous story of Job. Job 1:6 says, "One day the heavenly beings came to present themselves before the Lord, and Satan also came among them." Notice that Satan is not hunkered down in an enemy command post sending out demonic troops. Satan is standing in the heavenly court before God as a kind of district attorney. Satan's role is to convince God that people should be condemned and destroyed.

In verse 8 the Lord says to Satan, "Have you considered my servant Job? There is no one like him on the earth, a blameless and upright man who fears God and turns away from evil."

Why would God say such a thing to Satan? Because Satan is the prosecutor who wants to prove that humans are hopelessly corrupt, and Job is God's evidence against that assertion. Job is good and just, proving that humans are not as hopelessly corrupt as Satan suggests.

But Satan scoffs, "Does Job fear God for nothing? Look at everything you have given to him. But take it all away, and then watch how he treats you." Satan wants to show that faced with unspeakable suffering, Job will become as bitter and hate-filled as everyone else.

The rest of story is a test to see if Satan is right. Will Job still want a relationship with God even after suffering tragedy and disease?

The second Old Testament use of Satan as a proper name comes in Zechariah 3. Verse 1 says, "Then he [an angel] showed me the high priest Joshua standing before the angel of the Lord, and Satan standing at his right hand to accuse him." Note the similarity to the story of Job. Satan stands in the heavenly court to accuse human beings before God.

In this instance Satan has a good case. Verse 3: "Now Joshua was dressed with filthy clothes as he stood before the angel." In the Bible filthy clothes are a symbol for sin. Filthy clothes mean that the evidence against Joshua is overwhelming. But an angel intervenes. Verse 4: "The angel said to those who were standing before him, 'Take off his filthy clothes.' And to him [Joshua] he said, 'See, I have taken away your guilt from you, and I will clothe you with festal apparel.'" In this story Satan's case against Joshua is dismissed, not because Satan lacks evidence, but because God grants Joshua a full pardon.

There is only one other place in the Old Testament where Satan is mentioned by name: I Chronicles 21:1—"Satan stood up against Israel and incited David to count the people of Israel." In today's practice of law this would be called "entrapment." Satan is tempting David to do something wrong—something God did not want David to do—so that David's actions can be used to condemn him. Here, too, Satan is acting in the role of prosecutor. But this time Satan tempts people to do evil so that their evil can be used as evidence against them.

This also fits with the portrayal of the serpent in Genesis 3. The serpent in Genesis 3 is not called Satan, but it functions like Satan—tempting Adam and Eve to break God's commandment so that God will condemn them.

Now we come to the New Testament. The gospels mention Satan 14 times. Sometimes Satan is pictured as tempting Jesus, just as Satan did to Adam and Eve (Matthew 4:10, 16:23; Mark 1:13, 8:33) or planting in Judas the idea of betraying Jesus (Luke 22:3; John 13:27). In another case Satan is pictured as taking away the word of Jesus from our hearts (Mark 4:15). More dramatic, however, are the references to Jesus defeating Satan (Matthew 12:26, Mark 3:23-26, Luke 10:18). How does Jesus defeat Satan?

The best place to see this is in Revelation 12. In this highly symbolic story, a dragon pursues a woman in order to devour her child as soon as it is born. While the identity of the woman is confusing, there is no question about the identity of the child. He is Jesus. After the dragon fails to devour Jesus, a war breaks out in heaven between the dragon and the angels. The dragon is defeated and thrown down out of heaven. At this point the dragon is finally identified: "The great dragon was thrown down, that ancient serpent [probably a reference to the serpent in the Garden of Eden], who is called the Devil and Satan" (Revelation 12:9). Here Revelation uses both the Greek and Hebrew words for this ancient prosecutor against humanity.

Then comes a shout of joy—verse 10: "I heard a loud voice in heaven, proclaiming, 'Now have come the salvation and the power and the kingdom of our God and the authority of his Messiah, for the accuser of our comrades has been thrown down, who accuses them night and day before our God.'" Note again the Bible's pictures of Satan as an accuser—a prosecutor standing in heaven to accuse God's people.

So what does it mean that Satan has been thrown out of heaven? It means his case has been thrown out of court. God's people have been declared not guilty.[4] Why? Verse 11: "But they have conquered him by the blood of the Lamb and by the word of their testimony." Satan's case against humanity has been dismissed because Jesus died for us on the cross, and we are witnesses of that good news.

This plays out symbolically during the climactic battle in the book of Revelation. Riding a white horse, a figure enters the battle whose name is "The Word of God"—clearly a symbol for Jesus. This warrior wins the battle with a sharp sword coming out of his *mouth* (Revelation 19:13-16). The picture of a sword coming out of Jesus' mouth is not a symbol of military power, but of truth. The lies of Satan are defeated by the truth of the gospel.

When the dragon is thrown out of heaven, it makes war on the woman and the rest of her offspring. What does this mean? Consider the situation: Satan's case against us has been thrown out of the heavenly court. If Satan has failed to convince God that humans are hopeless and should be destroyed, then Satan's only recourse is to make *people* think that humans are hopeless and should be destroyed. If Satan cannot convince God to destroy us, then Satan must convince us to destroy one another.

And that is the power of Satan in the world. Movies like *The Exorcist* have nothing to do with the Bible. In the Bible, Satan's only real power is the power of a lie, the insinuation—notice how the word "sin" is embedded in that word—the in*sin*uation that human beings are irredeemable and should be destroyed.

In saying this, I do not mean to minimize the destructive power of Satan. Satan has no power over us except the power to make us believe a lie. But that lie can be horribly destructive. The Holocaust in Nazi Germany was the product of Satan's lie: that Jewish people are evil and should be destroyed. Slavery in America was also the product of Satan's lie: that people from Africa are not real human beings and can be treated like property. Satan's lie is reproduced every day through terrorism, bombing, exploitation, and tyranny. We see it in civil wars from Syria to Nigeria. It manifests itself in school shootings, gun battles, domestic violence, sex trafficking, and children bullied by their classmates.

But God gives us the Holy Spirit to expose that lie. As Jesus says in John 14, the Holy Spirit is our Advocate. If Satan is the prosecutor, the Holy Spirit is our witness for the defense. The apostle Paul says, "It is that very Spirit bearing witness with our spirit that we are children of God" (Romans 8:16). Note again the courtroom language. The Holy Spirit bears witness that people have worth. Jesus proved that beyond a reasonable doubt on the cross. The Holy Spirit bears witness that people are redeemable. God proved that by raising the Jesus from the dead. The Holy Spirit bears witness that we belong in God's presence. It proved that by calling us into the family of God known as the church.

In Ephesians, chapter 6, the apostle Paul says, "Put on the whole armor of God, so that you may be able to stand against the wiles of the devil" (Ephesians 6:11). Then he lists the kinds of armor he has in mind:

- Fasten the belt of truth around your waist.
- Put on the breastplate of righteousness.
- As shoes for your feet put on whatever will make you ready to proclaim the gospel of peace.
- Take the shield of faith, with which you will be able to quench all the flaming arrows of the evil one.
- Take the helmet of salvation, and the sword of the Spirit, which is the word of God (Ephesians 6:14-17).

All of these images speak of faith in the truth of the gospel. The lies of the devil are defeated by our trust in God's love for us as shown in the life, death, and resurrection of Jesus.

Who Will Be Saved?

At this point I must address what for many people is the most troubling objection to the Christian faith: Do we really think that only Christians will be saved? What about all those who grew up never knowing about Jesus? Or what about those who grew up hearing about Jesus from people they could not stand? Isn't faith in Jesus a consequence of birth and circumstance?

Here is the key point: to say that we are saved by Jesus does not mean only Christians will be saved. The Bible is quite exclusive when it comes to *how* we are saved. We are not saved by good works, education, legislation, or therapy (recall chapter 3). We are saved by Jesus' death for us on a cross and his resurrection from the dead, which is a first installment on God's new creation.

But *who* is saved? That is another matter. The Bible makes tantalizingly open statements about this. Jesus says, "I have other sheep that do not belong to this fold. I must bring them also, and they will listen to my voice. So there will be one flock, one shepherd" (John 10:16). In the context of Jesus' earthly life, he is probably talking about how Gentiles will be included in Jesus' family. But whom else might this include? We don't know.

Later the apostle Paul talks about how God brings the gospel to Gentiles in order that non-believing Jews may also be drawn to Jesus (Romans 11:11-32). How exactly does this work? We don't know. But Paul concludes the discussion by saying, "For God has imprisoned all in disobedience so that he may be merciful to all" (Romans 11:32). Who is included in the word "all"? We don't know.

We cannot say who will be saved, only how. We will be saved by the grace of the Lord Jesus Christ, and the proper response to this good news is not pride but gratitude.

The New Creation

But what about the world? What about God's beloved creation? I mentioned earlier the vision of Revelation 21—the creation of a new heaven and earth, where death and suffering will be no more, and God will wipe every tear from our eyes.

The last chapter of the Bible, Revelation 22, expands on this vision:

Then the angel showed me the river of the water
of life, bright as crystal, flowing from the throne
of God and of the Lamb through the middle of the
street of the city. On either side of the river, is the
tree of life with its twelve kinds of fruit, producing
its fruit each month; and the leaves of the tree are for
the healing of the nations. Nothing accursed will be
found there any more. But the throne of God and of
the Lamb will be in it, and his servants will worship
him (Revelation 22:1-3).

In the end creation is not destroyed but redeemed. The
tree of life, lost in Genesis 3, is restored. The world was
created good, but because of human sin it became a place of
guilt, suffering, conflict, and destruction. God's answer to
this is not to destroy the creation in a cosmic conflagration,
but to transform it into the place it was meant to be all along,
inhabited by people loving God, loving one another, and
caring for the world.

Jonathan Kozol spent a year interviewing children
and families in one of the poorest congressional districts
in America: the South Bronx of New York. He describes
the neighborhood as comprising mostly squalid buildings:
freezing in winter, humid in summer, and crawling with rats
that terrify infants in their cribs.

Over the course of the year he got to know a 12 year-old
boy named Anthony, an acolyte at the neighborhood Catholic
Church. One day they were talking about the plagues in
Egypt at the time of Moses, and Anthony said, "The plague
of Egypt is, of course, not over. It's over in Egypt but it could
have gone to other places. Plagues are never really over.
They can move from place to place."

Kozol asked him to describe such plagues, and Anthony
said, "Sadness is one plague today. Desperate would be a
plague. Drugs are a plague also, but the one who gets it does
not have to be the firstborn. It can be the second son. It could
be the youngest."

Kozol then asks Anthony when he thinks the plagues
will end. Anthony says, "I don't know when. I think it will

happen only in the kingdom of heaven, but even the angels do not know when that will come. I only know that this [gesturing to his neighborhood] is not His kingdom."[5]

Anthony, the church acolyte, is delivering good Christian theology. This world is not the way it is supposed to be. It is a place of pain, and that is not what its Creator ultimately wants for us.

Later Kozol asks Anthony to describe what God's kingdom will be like. In response Anthony writes an essay about it:

> God's Kingdom. God will be there. He'll be happy that we have arrived. People shall come hand-in-hand. It will be bright, not dim and glooming like on earth. All friendly animals will be there, but no mean ones. As for television, forget it! If you want vision, you can use your eyes to see the people that you love. No one will look at you from the outside. People will see you from the inside. All the people from the street will be there. My uncle will be there and he will be healed. You won't see him buying drugs, because there won't be money. Mr. Mongo will be there too. You might see him happy for a change. ... No violence will there be in heaven. There will be no guns or drugs or IRS. You won't have to pay taxes. You'll recognize all the children who have died when they were little. Jesus will be good to them and play with them. At night he'll come and visit at your house.[6]

I was struck by the "worldliness" of Anthony's picture. The kingdom of God does not mean the destruction of human bodily life, but its transformation. And whatever we do to anticipate that transformation, or give people glimpses of it, will be incorporated into that new creation.

Jesus said, "Blessed are those who hunger and thirst for righteousness, for they will be filled" (Matthew 5:6). We are not supposed to be satisfied with the world as it is. Believing in Jesus' resurrection means believing that the new creation is going to win. And whenever we feed the hungry, help the homeless, comfort the sorrowing, or provide medical care to the sick—whenever we work to make people's lives better in this physical earthly world—we bear witness to how important this world is to God and how determined God is to redeem it.

Questions for Discussion

1. What is your picture of heaven, or the kingdom of God? What about it is similar to our lives here and now? What is different?
2. What is your picture of hell? What would be "hell" for you?
3. Where in history have we seen certain categories of people labeled evil—fit only for destruction? Where do we see that today? What is needed to combat those labels?
4. What is the connection between grace and judgment? How could judgment be a vindication of God's love?

9

Hope and Courage

People sometimes picture God as "over" us—the Almighty Creator far above our ability to comprehend. Or they picture God as "within" us—the Force, the Ground of Being, who suffuses all of life. The Bible shares these images, but adds another. In the Bible, God is "ahead" of us, going before us into the future. Thus God "led" the people of Israel through the wilderness out of oppression in Egypt and into the Promised Land. And Jesus told his disciples, "In my Father's house are many dwelling places. If it were not so, would I have told you that I go to prepare a place for you? And if I go and prepare a place for you, I will come again and take you to myself, so that where I am, there you may be also" (John 14:2-3).

Theologian Jurgen Moltmann writes,

> *Future* is not just something or other to do with Christianity. It is the essential element of the faith which is specifically Christian: the keynote of all it hymns, the dawn colouring of the new day in which everything is bathed. For faith is Christian faith when it is *Easter* faith. Faith means living in the presence of the risen Christ, and stretching out to the coming kingdom of God. It is in the creative expectation of Christ's coming that our everyday experiences of life take place. We wait and hasten, we hope and endure, we pray and watch, we are both patient and curious. That makes the Christian life exciting and alive.[1]

It also gives us courage.

The Connection between Hope and Courage

The apostle Paul was no stranger to adversity. He tells the Corinthians he has some kind of "thorn in the flesh," probably some kind of physical ailment (II Corinthians 12:7). He also endured "afflictions, hardships, calamities, beatings, imprisonments, riots, labors, sleepless nights, and hunger" (II Corinthians 6:4-5), not to mention that once he was nearly stoned to death and on three occasions he was shipwrecked (II Corinthians 11:25). Yet he tells the Corinthians:

> We are afflicted in every way, but not crushed; perplexed, but not driven to despair; persecuted, but not forsaken; struck down, but not destroyed; always carrying in the body the death of Jesus, so that the life of Jesus may also be made visible in our mortal bodies (II Corinthians 4:8-10).

In each of these comparisons the key element is hope. To be afflicted but not crushed means to have hope. To be perplexed but not driven to despair means to have hope. It means to believe that God is not yet finished. Hence Paul tells the Corinthians, "We know that the one who raised the Lord Jesus will raise us also with Jesus, and will bring us with you into his presence" (II Corinthians 4:14).

Leslie, a member of the church I currently serve in Des Moines, Washington, shared a personal testimony at one of our Easter services. Prior to this she had attended an adult education class at our church where I answered questions about life after death and the Christian belief in the resurrection. In response to questions about what life in the resurrection might be like, I read Paul's response to the Corinthians:

> But someone will ask, "How are the dead raised? With what kind of body do they come?" Fool! What you sow does not come to life unless it dies. And as for what you sow, you do not sow the body that is to be, but a bare seed, perhaps of wheat or some other

grain. But God gives it a body as he has chosen, and to each kind of seed its own body (I Corinthians 15:35-38).

I read this scripture to indicate that we cannot speculate about the kind of body we will have in the resurrection, any more than one who has never seen a pine tree can imagine one from looking at a pine cone.

But Leslie saw a deeper meaning in this scripture, an image that connected to her own experience of new life growing out of times of discouragement and depression. So she wrote a poem about it which she shared with our church on Easter, calling it *"Lament of a Seed."*

Cries a seed, "I'm at my end! Dried up, useless.
　　Escaped from those seeking to devour me only to
　　arrive here. Cruel fate, you prove cruel to the bitter
　　end!"
Comforts a gardener, "Take courage, you are beginning."
Cries a seed, "I am perishing! Look, see: I am now
　　buried. Earth covers, crushes."
Assures a gardener, "Take courage, you are found."
Cries a seed, "I am lost! Covered, hidden. And now
　　here is the rain! I will be drowned."
Sooths a gardener, "Take courage, you are remembered."
Cries a seed, "I am forgotten! Burning now with heat
　　from the sun, here in my shallow grave."
Affirms a gardener: "Take courage, you are redeemed."
Cries a seed, "I am forsaken!"
Cries a seed, "I am frightened!"
Cries a seed, "I am broken! My very flesh, split! My
　　end is here, I am finished."
Whispers a gardener, "Take courage, I am here."
Quietly notices a seed, "You…are here. And me? I
　　am…here…too? And I am…growing? … What is
　　this new flesh, previously unimaginable? It is…
　　exquisite. Supple, thriving. … Is this really me? …
　　Yes, I feel it, certain of the taste of life."

Declares a seed, to the gardener, "I thought I lived
before, but no. My dwelling was a cave. I am
emerged. This world is different but I see that it is
Good. What strange passage: I thought I died. I am
utterly alive."
*Smiles the Gardener: "Welcome, dear one. Take heart, rejoice:
this is merely the beginning of glory."*[2]

Here is the connection between courage and hope. In a
short poem called "Courage," Karle Wilson Baker writes,

Courage is armor
A blind man wears,
The calloused scar
Of outlived despairs:
Courage is fear
That has said its prayers.[3]

Courage is fear that has said its prayers. Or to put it
another way, courage grows out of the faith that God is going
before us, leading us into a new future.

A Faith to Die For

The apostle Paul wrote the letter to the Philippians from
jail. We don't know why he was imprisoned, but undoubtedly
it stemmed from the message he preached about Jesus. Yet
he is remarkably positive about his situation:

I want you to know, beloved, that what has happened
to me has actually helped to spread the gospel, so that
it has become known throughout the whole imperial
guard and to everyone else that my imprisonment
is for Christ; and most of the brothers and sisters,
having been made confident in the Lord by my
imprisonment, dare to speak the word with greater
boldness and without fear (Philippians 1:12-14).

Paul's imprisonment has given courage to other believers
as they share their faith, and even the guards have been
exposed to it.

But from where does Paul's courage come? He answers that question in Philippians, chapter 3:

"But our citizenship is in heaven, and it is from there that we are expecting a Savior, the Lord Jesus Christ. He will transform the body of our humiliation that it may be conformed to the body of his glory, by the power that also enables him to make all things subject to himself (Philippians 3:20-21).

Paul is not looking for an escape from bodily life into heaven. He is looking for a Savior who will come from heaven to transform bodily life. And the goal of that transformation is not just the salvation of Paul but the salvation of all things—making all things subject to Christ. Paul has courage because he has hope. He knows that God is going to win.

At the age of 86 a bishop of the early church named Polycarp was arrested for refusing to acknowledge the deity of Caesar and instead proclaiming that Jesus was the one true Lord. When the governor threatened execution if he did not renounce Christ, Polycarp replied, "Eighty-six years I have served him, and he never did me wrong. How can I blaspheme my King who has saved me?" He was then sentenced to burning at the stake, but just before the logs were lit, he said this prayer:

Lord God Almighty, Father of thy beloved and blessed Servant Jesus Christ, through whom we have received full knowledge of thee, the God of angels and powers and all creation and of the whole race of the righteous who live in thy presence: I bless thee, because thou hast deemed me worthy of this day and hour, to take my part in the number of the martyrs, in the cup of thy Christ, for resurrection to eternal life of soul and body in the immortality of the Holy Spirit.[4]

In this short prayer Polycarp summarizes the faith we have been talking about: that the God who created the world has been revealed to us in Jesus, and that through his resurrection we have been invited into a new creation, a transformation of body and soul, of which in this life we are imperfect witnesses—the original meaning of the Greek word *martyr*. For Polycarp such a faith was worth sacrificing his life, especially if the alternative meant worshiping a power hungry Roman emperor.

Many other early followers of Jesus had to decide if their faith was worth dying for. There is a remarkable journal written by Perpetua, a woman who lived in Carthage around the year 200. We know that Perpetua was highly educated, because she wrote fluently in Latin. Her journal is one of the few writings from the early church unquestionably written by a woman. Perpetua became a follower of Jesus when she was 20 years old. Shortly before her baptism she was arrested and thrown in prison for refusing to offer sacrifices to the Roman emperor. She writes,

> While I was still with the police authorities my father out of love for me tried to dissuade me from my resolution. "Father," I said, "do you see here, for example, this vase, or pitcher, or whatever it is?" "I see it," he said. "Can it be named anything else than what it really is?" I asked, and he said, "No." "So I also cannot be called anything else than what I am, a Christian."

Finally she was brought to trial before Hilarion, the Roman governor of Carthage. She continues in her journal:

> Hilarion said, "Have pity on your father's gray head; ... offer sacrifice for the emperor's welfare." But I answered, "I will not." Hilarion asked, "Are you a Christian?" And I answered, "I am a Christian." ... Then the sentence was passed; all of us were condemned to the beasts.[5]

For Perpetua, as for Polycarp and many others, the Christian faith was worth dying for.

In a short documentary called *The Presbyterians*, an African American pastor is shown working with a group of children at an inner city church in Pittsburgh. During their prayer time, one of the children says, "My mother needs a job." Another says, "I need a father. I don't have a father and I hate kids who have fathers." So they pray about these things. They close by saying together the Apostles' Creed, all of them reciting it from memory. After the meeting the pastor is interviewed, and she says, "I feel like I'm in a struggle. Good and bad—sometimes it's great, sometimes it's not. But I never think of giving up. Because if you haven't found something to die for, you have not lived."

If you haven't found something to die for, you have not lived. The Christian faith is worth dying for, because it is a faith worth living for, especially when the alternative is despair.

A Promise Not Fulfilled in our Lifetime

The courage to continue serving God even in the face of death comes in part from the knowledge that God's work may not be finished in our lifetime.

This is a recurring theme in the Bible. Abraham was promised a land that his descendants would inherit and where they would become a great nation, bringing blessing to all the families of the earth (Genesis 12:1-3). With that promise Abraham moved to the land of Canaan and lived there as a sojourner—a resident alien. During his lifetime the only piece of the Promised Land he actually owned was the burial plot for his wife Sarah. He lived for a promise not fulfilled in his lifetime.

So did Moses. For 40 years Moses led the people of Israel, liberating them from slavery in Egypt, leading them through the wilderness, and finally bringing them to the border of Canaan, the land promised to his ancestor Abraham. On this journey Moses faced three wars, two major rebellions, a famine, two droughts, and a plague. Finally, they came to the Jordan River, ready to cross into the Promised Land. But God said to Moses, "Sorry, you can't go in. You will die here in the wilderness." God allowed Moses to see the Promised Land from the top of Mt. Nebo, but he died before setting foot in it.

Why this happened is never clearly explained. Some passages of the Bible suggest that Moses disobeyed a command of God, but if so, the actual command is unclear. Moses himself suggests that God holds him responsible for the disobedience of the people. We don't really know why Moses died before entering the Promised Land, but there is a lesson in this story. Servants of Jesus often end up like Moses, giving their lives for a mission they do not see fulfilled in their lifetime.

In chapter 1 I told the story of the Vacation Bible School teacher I had when I was 7 years old. During that week of Vacation Bible School she helped me experience God's personal care for me and led me in a prayer to accept Jesus into my life, even though at the time I did not really understand what that meant. Like the commitment of marriage, it is something you understand only after you have been in it a long time.

After the week of Vacation Bible School, I never saw that teacher again. By the end of the summer my father was transferred to another Air Force base, and we moved. I don't even remember her name. This teacher who helped put Jesus into my boat—speaking metaphorically as well as literally—never saw what happened to her little student, or how his life turned out. She was like Moses, like countless other Sunday School teachers, youth leaders, pastors, and people in churches. She never saw the results of her effort. But one day she will.

Like Moses we live for a promise that may not be fulfilled in our lifetime. We serve a mission whose fruits may not be seen for generations. And yet because of our faith, we know that our labor will not be in vain.

The most famous sermon about Moses on Mt. Nebo was delivered on April 3, 1968. It was given not in a church but at a rally of sanitation workers in Memphis, TN. They were on strike for higher pay and safer working conditions. The strike began in February of that year after two sanitation workers were crushed to death by machinery. In the months that followed, the strike came to be associated with the civil rights movement, since most of the sanitation workers were African American. On April 3, Martin Luther King, Jr. addressed the striking workers and ended with this allusion to Moses on Mt. Nebo:

> Well, I don't know what will happen now. We've got some difficult days ahead. But it really doesn't matter …because I've been to the mountaintop. … I've seen the Promised Land. I may not get there with you. But I want you to know tonight, that we as a people will get to the Promised Land. And so I'm happy tonight. I'm not worried about anything. I'm not fearing any man. Mine eyes have seen the glory of the coming of the Lord.

The next day, April 4, King was assassinated on a motel balcony in Memphis.

Karl Marx dismissed religion, specifically Christianity, as the "opiate of the people." But far from being a drug that makes people insensitive to injustice and suffering, the Christian faith has historically given people courage to confront these issues, unafraid of death threats or even chronically discouraging results. They know that God is not yet finished, even though they might not see the final outcome during their earthly lives.

Harriet Beecher Stowe bears witness to this through her hero in the book *Uncle Tom's Cabin*. Toward the end of the novel Simon Legree, the slave owner, orders Tom to beat another slave into submission. But Tom refuses. He says, "I'm willing to work night and day, and work while there's life and breath in me; but this yer thing I can't feel it right to do; and, Mas'r, I *never* shall do it,—*never!*"

Simon Legree says to Tom, "What! ye blasted black beast! tell *me* ye don't think it *right* to do what I tell ye! What have any of you cussed cattle to do with thinking what's right? … Ain't I yer master? Didn't I pay down twelve hundred dollars, cash, for all there is inside yer old cussed black shell? An't yer mine, now, body and soul?" And he gave Tom a violent kick with his heavy boot.

"No! no! no! my soul ain't yours, Mas'r!" said Tom. "You haven't bought it,—ye can't buy it! It's been bought and paid for, by the one that is able to keep it;—no matter, no matter, you can't harm me!"

"I can't!" said Legree with a sneer; "we'll see,—we'll see!" And Legree orders two of his slave drivers to beat Tom into unconsciousness.

But the next day Tom still won't obey Simon's order to beat one of the other slaves. He says to Simon, "Mas'r, I know ye can do dreadful things, but after ye've killed the body, there ain't no more ye can do. And oh, there's all ETERNITY to come, after that!"[6]

When we fear God, we need not fear death or futility. Because when we seek first God's kingdom and God's justice, we know that our labor will not be in vain.

Faith, Courage, and Purpose

How does faith look in a prison camp? During the Nazi occupation of Holland, Corrie ten Boom and her family harbored Jews in their home, motivated by a deep Christian conviction that they must resist the Nazi attempts to exterminate them. But eventually they were discovered and arrested. Corrie and her sister Betsie were sent to a camp for political prisoners at Vught. Arriving after an exhausting day of travel and miles of marching to reach the camp, they stood for hours waiting to be processed and listening to a camp matron recite the rules. Corrie ten Boom describes the scene in her book *The Hiding Place*:

> We followed the officer down a wide street lined with barracks on either side and halted at one of the gray, featureless sheds. It was the end of the long day of standing, waiting, hoping. ... And still we were not allowed to sit: there was a last wait while the matron with maddening deliberateness checked off our documents against a list. "Betsie!" I wailed, "how long will it take?"

"Perhaps a long, long time," Betsie replied. "Perhaps many years. But what better way could there be to spend our lives?"

I turned to stare at her. "Whatever are you talking about?"

"These young women," Betsie replied. "That girl back at the bunkers. Corrie, if people can be taught to hate, they can be taught to love! We must find the way, you and I, no matter how long it takes."[7]

Far from causing us to dismiss the world or cease caring about it, Christian hope, rightly understood, gives us the courage to share Christ's love in the world, because we know that love will eventually win, even in us.

I have never been threatened with arrest or death for preaching about Jesus. For that reason, in this chapter I have focused less on my own story and more on the lives of people who have faced much greater challenges and dangers than I have. However, you cannot serve in ministry for a long period of time without beginning to wonder if it really makes a difference in anyone's life. A lot of ministry is like the work of my Vacation Bible School teacher: an investment whose results may not be seen in our lifetime. But every so often I have received glimpses of God's power to transform lives, and that has kept me going.

At one of the churches I served, there was a young woman who grew up in the church youth group. She went on one of our mission trips to Mexico to build a small house for a homeless family. Partly because of that experience, she studied Spanish and after college went to work with a Christian organization operating orphanages in Latin America. She worked at orphanages in Honduras and El Salvador, and then became the director of an orphanage in Bolivia. At first, her experience with suffering children almost destroyed her faith. How could a loving God allow children to suffer? That question has already been asked several times in this book. But gradually she came to a new understanding of how God works in our lives. She sent me a long email including these words:

> I was in El Salvador when I started truly believing again. And it was partly because in the midst of complete despair, there was still hope. It was as if I finally stopped asking, "If there is a God, why does all this suffering exist?" and I started being awed by the way God was touching people's hearts to ease suffering and give hope where it seemed there could be none. I stopped expecting things to be perfect and fair, and I learned to live with the longing for something better. I learned to accompany people in their suffering and accept that there was little I could do for them other than be there. And gradually I learned that being there was pretty important! ...
>
> It's been a journey. I still have so many questions, and I probably always will. There will always be experiences that threaten to weaken our faith— frustrations, doubts, anger—at having to pay a bill before a child can be admitted to the ER, a teenager on the street corner with her baby sniffing glue, the old man sitting on the highway in the middle of 3 lanes of busy traffic begging for help, children so weak with hunger their hair is changing colors and they can't even hold your gaze. These experiences, sights, smells will forever be a part of my consciousness, and I am glad, because they make me more human and keep me from wasting energy on things that aren't important. They allow me to see Jesus in the faces of the suffering, and just try to love them. And so I no longer question if God exists, because I know he does.

This is not an intellectual argument; it is an invitation to a way of life. And in the process of living that life, the faith on which it is based becomes more real and powerful, not only in shaping our own lives but in touching the lives of people around us.

That's why I invite you to believe. In the final chapter I will talk about how to believe.

Questions for Discussion

1. What keeps you going? Or more specifically, what gives you courage to keep doing the things you believe God wants you to do?
2. Who in your past has done important things for you and invested in your life but did not live to see how your life turned out? What do you think motivated them?
3. When in your life have you seen yourself as a dying seed? When have you seen yourself as a shoot that was sprouting, or a plant that was thriving? What made those transitions possible?
4. What makes it easy or hard to see God's purpose for your life?

10

How to Believe

In the introduction I mentioned the conversation I had with my high school debate partner Mike. I told Mike I believe in God because I think that we are not alone in the world, that we are put here for a purpose and that we are loved. His reaction surprised me. He said, "I wish I could believe that."

It would be nice to end this book by describing how Mike found a new faith in God that changed his life. But the truth is that I don't know what happened with Mike's faith. After high school we went to different colleges, pursued different career paths, moved to opposite sides of the country, and lost touch. There was no Facebook or even internet in those days, and we were both too busy to correspond. Then, a few years ago, I heard from another high school friend that Mike had died.

So I cannot report what happened with Mike's search for faith. Hopefully God brought people into his life who helped him with that search better than I did in high school.

Looking back, however, I realize that Mike needed more than an answer to the question of why to believe. He was struggling with how to believe. How do you have Christian faith when you have trouble believing some or all of its central tenets? So now, in this last chapter I will try to answer the question I did not realize Mike was asking: not why believe, but how?

Faith Mixed with Doubt

Kristen is a poster child for faith and doubt—or more precisely, a poster teenager. She was interviewed as part of the National Study of Youth and Religion, a phone survey of 3,000 teenagers, followed by in-person interviews with 267 of them. Results of the study are described in the book *Soul Searching: The Religious and Spiritual Lives of American Teenagers*, by Christian Smith.

Kristen was 16 years-old when she was first interviewed. Her father had committed suicide. Kristen found his body on a bed with a self-inflicted gunshot wound to the head. Christian Smith said he expected Kristen to be another case of troubled family, traumatic loss, at-risk childhood, and bad teen outcomes. But Kristen's story did not go that way. She explained, "It was something tragic, and now when I look at it I'm just like, 'wow that was pretty bad,' and people were saying like we were going to go off the deep end and that we kids need counseling. But you know, God used it in a great way and to shape my mom."

Kristen explained that her father's suicide caused the whole family to take their faith more seriously: to pray more, read the Bible, and rely on God in a way they never had before. Christian Smith observed, "Although many would not share her conservative religious views, Kristen was nonetheless, as far as I could tell, simply a down-to-earth, fun, clear-thinking, religiously committed, generally impressive kid."

Later Smith asked her if she ever had doubts about her faith. Kristen replied,

> I have. I have wondered if I'm really saved and if I died would I go to heaven and is there really a God. But even if there's not, I don't think there's anything else better to believe 'cause then you've lost hope. Sometimes I wonder, there's so many other religions and they all claim to be true and I claim mine to be true and so, you know, what's right? And then I think, whatever it is, [Christianity] is the best that I've heard.[1]

In Matthew's gospel, after the resurrection, Jesus sends word to his eleven remaining disciples to meet him in Galilee. Matthew says, "Now the eleven disciples went to Galilee, to the mountain to which Jesus had directed them. When they saw him, they worshiped him; but some doubted" (Matthew 28:16-17).

Even after seeing Jesus risen from the dead, some still doubted! Nothing in this book or any book can erase all doubt. Dale Bruner, one of my teachers at Whitworth University, told a group of us, "God reveals enough of himself to make faith possible, and conceals enough to make faith necessary."

Doubt is not antithetical to faith; it is a corollary. Without the possibility or even the presence of doubt, faith would not be faith. It would be something more like arrogant self-confidence, of which Christians have been too often guilty.

In his book *Blue Like Jazz* Donald Miller writes,

> The goofy thing about Christian faith is that you believe it and don't believe it at the same time. ... I believe in Jesus; I believe He is the Son of God, but every time I sit down to explain this to somebody I feel like a palm reader, like somebody who works at a circus or a kid who is always making things up or somebody at a Star Trek convention who hasn't figured out that the show isn't real.[2]

You can believe in the Christian faith and doubt it at the same time, just as Jesus' disciples did. And yet the disciples went to Galilee looking for Jesus, even if they had doubts about seeing him. And because they went, despite their doubts, they met Jesus and became his apostles.

A similar story is told in the gospel of John. Thomas was not present with the other disciples when Jesus appeared to them after his resurrection. They told Thomas about it, but Thomas said, "Unless I see the mark of the nails in his hands, and put my finger in the mark of the nails and my hand in his side, I will not believe" (John 20:25). For this he has earned the nickname "Doubting Thomas."

Yet Doubting Thomas came back the next week when the disciples gathered again. This gathering of disciples on Sunday, one week after Easter, began a pattern most Christian churches still follow: gathering for worship on the first day of the week in remembrance of Jesus' resurrection and as a testimony to the beginning of a new creation. Thomas may have had doubts about Jesus, but on the first Sunday after Easter he showed up at "church" with the other disciples, and in the process he met the Risen Lord.

Later in his discussion of faith Donald Miller tells about a conversation he had with a friend from Reed College named Laura. Laura came to him obviously distraught. She said,

> "I feel like He is after me, Don."
> "Who is after you?" I asked.
> "God." ...
> "What do you think He wants?"
> "I don't know. I can't do this, Don. You don't under-
>   stand. I can't do this."
> "Can't do what, Laura?"
> "Be a Christian."
> "Why can't you be a Christian?"
> Laura didn't say anything. She just looked at me and
>   rolled her tired eyes. ... "There is this part of me
>   that wants to believe. I wrote about it in my journal.
>   My family believes, Don. I feel as though I need to
>   believe. Like I am going to die if I don't believe. But
>   it is all so stupid. So completely stupid."
> "Laura, why is it that you hang out with Christians on
>   campus?"
> "I don't know. I guess I am just curious."[3]

Laura reminds me of the disciples. Why did the disciples go to Galilee? Why did Thomas come to the prayer meeting that night? Maybe they were just curious. So they followed Jesus, despite their doubts, and that is when Jesus became real to them.

Faith as Premise

Faith is less about certainty and more about the basic values and commitments on which you choose to base your life. It is less a matter of proof and more a matter of premise.

I learned about Euclid's fifth postulate in high school geometry. A postulate is an axiom or assumption from which other geometric ideas can be proved. In the form I learned it, Euclid's fifth postulate said that if a straight line intersected two other straight lines, both at a 90 degree angle, the other two lines would never meet; they would be parallel.

There have been many attempts to prove this postulate using Euclid's other four postulates, but none have been successful. Euclid's parallel postulate must be accepted as a premise.

With that premise Euclid produced an entire field of geometry, called Euclidean geometry. It proved very useful for describing how geometry works on a flat plane, but it was not as helpful for describing the interaction of geometric figures on a sphere. For example, on a sphere if you draw a line at a 90 degree angle from the equator going north, and then move to another spot on the equator and draw another line at a 90 degree angle going north, those two lines will eventually meet at the North Pole. They are not parallel. For describing lines and shapes on a sphere, it is more helpful to base your geometry on a different postulate than Euclid's.

The Christian faith is less like a geometric proof and more like a postulate. It is not something you can prove using different first principles; it is itself the first principle from which you derive other principles.

Philip Yancey describes faith as paranoia in reverse. He writes,

A paranoid person orients life around fear. My wife worked for a supervisor who became convinced, wrongly, that Janet had eyes on his job. Every suggestion Janet made at work, her supervisor took as an attempt to undermine him. Every compliment, he took as a subversive attempt to win him over.

Nothing Janet said could convince him otherwise, and eventually she had to leave the job to preserve her own sanity.

Faith, Yancey says, works the opposite of paranoia. It sees the events of life through the lens of trust in a loving God. He continues,

> A faithful person sees life from the perspective of trust, not fear. Bedrock faith allows me to believe that, despite the chaos of the present moment, God does reign; that regardless of how worthless I may feel, I truly matter to a God of love; that no pain lasts forever and no evil triumphs in the end. Faith sees even the darkest deed of all history, the death of God's Son, as a necessary prelude to the brightest.[4]

Neither the paranoid person nor the person of faith can be proven wrong. In that sense their viewpoints are like postulates. But one postulate leads to fear, and the other to hope. The latter, I submit, is the faith worth believing.

Faith as Decision

Gambling seems like an unlikely path to faith, but it was the path taken by the philosopher Blaise Pascal. In an essay called "The Wager," Pascal argues that God is so far beyond our comprehension we will never be able to prove God, nor disprove God. Therefore we must place a bet. We must decide whether to commit our lives to God or choose a world without God.

Pascal then engages in a kind of cost-benefit analysis. He writes,

> Let us weigh up the gain and the loss involved in calling heads that God exists. Let us assess the two cases: if you win you win everything, if you lose you lose nothing. Do not hesitate then; wager that [God] does exist.[5]

At a simple level, Pascal is weighing the possibility of eternal life against a choice that ultimately ends in death. He argues that the infinite blessing offered by choosing God more than outweighs the consequence of being wrong. For if God does not exist, you end up dead like everyone else. You lose nothing. But if God exists, your wager on God could mean eternal life.

Of course it is more complicated than that, for a wager on God means a lifetime of choices that may be different than the choices you would have made wagering against God. But even here Pascal argues that you really can't lose:

> Now what harm will come to you from choosing this course [to serve God]? You will be faithful, honest, humble, grateful, full of good works, a sincere, true friend. … It is true you will not enjoy noxious pleasures, glory and good living, but will you not have others? I tell you that you will gain even in this life, and that at every step you take along this road you will see that your gain is so certain and your risk so negligible that in the end you will realize that you have wagered on something certain and infinite for which you have paid nothing.[6]

Pascal comes to the same conclusion as Puddleglum, the Narnia character mentioned in the introduction. The Christian faith is worth believing even if it turns out not to be true.

During a church new member class, I visited with a class member who grew up in a Christian family. He told me, "I guess I am a Christian because my family was." I then asked him if he had ever questioned the faith of his parents. He thought for a moment, then said, "Yeah, when I was in college. In college I was around people who did not believe the things I had been taught about God growing up. And I realized that I was free to believe what I wanted to believe. So for a while I did not go to any church." "What brought you back?" I asked. He said, "I looked around at my friends who did not go to church and did not believe what I had been taught to believe, and I decided that I did not want to be like them. So I went back to church."

Another member in one of the churches I served was a young man who told of growing up with parents who showed little or no interest in the Christian faith, or in any other kind of faith. But he always had big "why" questions hovering over his head: "Why are we here? What is the reason for our existence?"

Then he met a young woman in our church and fell in love. He became attracted to the Christian faith because he saw how much it meant to her. He told a group of us at the church, "At that point it was a battle between my willingness to be ignorant and my eagerness to try something I never thought would come to define my life: to believe in someone greater than myself." He went on, "God is supposed to be the greatest part of a person's life, but I was denying him because he was inconvenient. It's almost as if I had decided he was real, but I had also decided that it was better that he stayed outside my personal bubble."

But after his marriage, he encountered a new perspective on God. At one point he hurt his wife deeply and felt shame—what he called "a deep pit of remorse and regret that made me feel too small to be of significance to anything or anyone." That's when he discovered not just a God of meaning but a God of grace. He told us,

> Soon after, I confessed to God and prayed for my wife, and a wonderful thing happened. Through her love and forgiveness God wrapped me up in a warm embrace assuring me that there was nothing that could defeat him. I so badly wanted trust and honesty to prevail in our marriage, but I realized for the first time in my life I had no means to accomplish this feat myself. I then entered into a lifelong fellowship with God. He was right there all along, just waiting.

A similar thing happened to Donald Miller's friend Laura. Despite her doubts, Laura remained curious about the Christian faith. So she hung out with other Christians on campus. Then she started reading the Bible. One morning she sent this email to Donald Miller:

> Dearest Friend Don, I read through the book of Matthew this evening. I was up all night. I couldn't stop reading so I read through Mark. This Jesus of yours is either a madman or the Son of God. Somewhere in the middle of Mark I realized he was the Son of God. I suppose that makes me a Christian. I feel much better now. Come to campus tonight and let's get coffee.[7]

The Christian faith has a kind of logic, as I have tried to explain in the chapters of this book. But in the end it is not the logic of the Christian faith which compels most people to believe it. It is the difference it makes in our lives when we choose to believe.

Faith as a Gift of Grace

I did not start college planning to get married before I went to seminary. To tell the truth, I fell in love. It was something that "happened" to me. Of course, when we became engaged, we both made a decision. No one held a gun to our heads, not even the proverbial shotgun. But looking back on it, I could not imagine doing anything else. I could not imagine choosing any other life, and still can't. So if you asked whether my marriage was a choice or a gift, I would say both.

The same thing is true for my faith. In one sense I chose to believe in Jesus, because I would rather follow someone like Jesus than any other savior the world might serve up. But in another sense, faith happened to me. I did not reason my way to the Christian faith, I fell in love with it, thanks to the caring people in my life who shared it with me. And the more I lived with that faith and learned about it and thought about it, the less I could imagine believing anything else.

Addressing the people of Israel after they escaped from slavery in Egypt and as they were about to enter the Promised Land, Moses says to them,

> I call heaven and earth to witness against you today that I have set before you life and death, blessings and curses. Choose life that you and your descendants may live, loving the Lord your God, obeying him, and holding fast to him (Deuteronomy 30:19-20).

In this scripture Moses calls the people of Israel to make a choice—to decide to follow God.

But in another part of Deuteronomy, Moses says to the people,

> For you are a people holy to the Lord your God; the Lord your God has chosen you out of all the peoples on earth to be his people, his treasured possession. It was not because you were more numerous than any other people that the LORD set his heart on you and chose you—for you were the fewest of all peoples. It was because the LORD loved you and kept the oath that he swore to your ancestors, that the Lord has brought you out with a mighty hand, and redeemed you from the house of slavery, from the hand of Pharaoh king of Egypt. (Deuteronomy 7:6-8).

Here Moses stresses how God chose Israel, not the other way around. So which is it? Is Israel's faith a choice or a gift? The answer is both.

The same is true for the disciples of Jesus. Early in John 15 Jesus says to the disciples, "Abide in me as I abide in you. Just as the branch cannot bear fruit by itself unless it abides in the vine, neither can you unless you abide in me" (John 15:4). In this verse the disciples are summoned to make a choice: to commit themselves to an on-going relationship with Jesus.

But then a few verses later Jesus says, "You did not choose me but I chose you. And I appointed you to go and bear fruit, fruit that will last, so that the Father will give you whatever you ask him in my name" (John 15:16). Is their relationship to Jesus a decision of the will or a gift of God's grace? The answer is both.

In his autobiography *Surprised by Joy* C. S. Lewis describes his own conversion to faith in terms of this same dynamic. He pictures God closing in on him, like chess pieces on a king. The chapter describing his conversion is called "Checkmate." In the process of describing his conversion, he makes this observation:

> The odd thing was that before God closed in on me, I was in fact offered what now appears a moment of wholly free choice. In a sense. ... I became aware that I was holding something at bay, or shutting something out. Or, if you like, that I was wearing some stiff clothing, like corsets, or even a suit of armor. ... I felt myself being, there and then, given a free choice. I could open the door or keep it shut; I could unbuckle the armor or keep it on. Neither choice was presented as a duty; no threat or promise was attached to either, though I knew that to open the door or to take off the corslet meant the incalculable. The choice appeared to be momentous but it was also strangely unemotional. I was moved by no desires or fears. In a sense I was not moved by anything. I chose to open, to unbuckle, to loosen the rein. I say, "I chose," yet it did not really seem possible to do the opposite.[8]

Faith is both a gift and a choice. This has four implications. First, because faith is a choice, we are responsible for our relationship with God. We may have had bad experiences in the past with hypocritical Christians or mean-spirited parents or lousy pastors, but we have the opportunity to make a new choice. Our heredity is not our destiny.

Second, because faith is a gift, we cannot brag about it. Being a follower of Jesus does not mean we are better than other people. We were chosen by God before we had done anything to deserve it. Our faith is a gift of grace, not a mark of superiority.

Third, because faith is a choice, we must maintain our commitment to it. People may fall in love, but marriage takes work. Commitment to a husband or wife is renewed by countless decisions made every day. The same is true for a relationship with God. When Jesus said, "Abide in me," he meant that discipleship is not a one-time decision; it is an on-going commitment. Our commitment to Jesus is renewed in daily decisions.

Fourth, because faith is a gift, the only proper response is gratitude. Since we cannot brag about our faith, we can only be grateful for it. And gratitude is a key to the life God wants us to live. The best antidote for depression is gratitude. The best antidote for resentment or bitterness is gratitude. The best antidote for greed or jealousy is gratitude. Gratitude expresses our realization that we have already been given the best gift anyone could have: a life of righteousness, joy, and peace in God's eternal kingdom, beginning in part here and now.

Faith as Practice

Earlier in this chapter I mentioned Pascal's wager of faith. But a wager on God is not a one-time decision. It is a decision that must be reaffirmed frequently if not daily. Pascal acknowledges this when he says that faith is not just a wager but a habit:

> For we must make no mistake about ourselves: we are as much automaton as mind. As a result, demonstration is not the only instrument for convincing us. How few things can be demonstrated! Proofs only convince the mind; habit provides the strongest proofs and those that are most believed.[9]

It is sometimes assumed that belief shapes behavior. But often it works the other way around. Behavior that is repeated and becomes ingrained can shape belief. In other words, we learn to believe by engaging regularly in the practices of belief.

This is central to my own story of faith. Despite our frequent moves, or perhaps because of them, my parents always sought out a church, and therefore I grew up with tangible reminders that God was with us wherever we went. And gradually it seeped into my consciousness that when I felt lonely because I had left my friends behind, I was not alone—God was there.

But it was not just going to church that gave me a sense of God's presence; it was the cumulative effect of all the songs I had learned in church, the stories I had been taught from the Bible, the Bible verses I had memorized, and even some sermons I heard. At the age of eleven, as I was wheeled into surgery to have my appendix removed, I remember specifically thinking of a Bible verse I had learned: "I can do all things through Christ who strengthens me" (Philippians 4:13). I kept saying that over and over to myself, and I felt reassured that I was in God's hands. And when we moved to a new place, and I worried about making friends and fitting in, I remembered another Bible verse: "Do not worry about anything, but in everything by prayer and supplication with thanksgiving let your requests be made known to God. And the peace of God, which surpasses all understanding, will guard your hearts and your minds in Christ Jesus" (Philippians 4:6-7).

This, in turn, encouraged me to pray, and as I practiced praying to God, I discovered that I could tell God all the things on my heart that I could not tell anyone else. It felt wonderful to be able to talk to God—to tell God how I felt when I was by myself in my room sobbing because I felt rejected by a friend. A psychologist could explain this as projection. It certainly bore similarities to what people do in classic psychoanalysis, lying on a couch talking to a therapist. But during those times of prayer, I felt that God heard, that God cared, that God reassured me, and sometimes I had the distinct feeling that God was making suggestions to me in the form of thoughts that came into my mind. I don't take seriously every thought that comes into my mind. But when I had thoughts that seemed a response to prayer, and when those thoughts seemed in keeping with the character of God as I had learned about it from reading the Bible and going to church, then I paid attention. And it made a difference in how I dealt with situations.

All of this happened long before I went to college and seminary. College and seminary were important because they helped me to understand what I had experienced and put it into the larger context of God's love for the world. But these experiences of God that shaped my faith did not come from theological reflection. They came from years of practicing faith before I really understood it.

In her book *Amazing Grace* Kathleen Norris describes the long and difficult process by which she came to embrace Christian faith. She writes, "But if I had to find one word to describe how belief came to take hold in me, it would be 'repetition.'" She then tells of a conversation between a seminary student and an Orthodox theologian at Yale Divinity School:

> The student's original question was centered on belief: "What can one do," he asked, "when one finds it impossible to affirm certain tenets of the Creed?" The priest responded, "Well, you just say it. It's not that hard to master. With a little effort, most can learn it by heart." ...
>
> The student, apparently feeling that he had been misunderstood, asked with some exasperation, "What am I to do...when I have difficulty affirming parts of the Creed—like the Virgin Birth?" And he got the same response. "You just say it. Particularly when you have difficulty believing it. You just keep saying it. It will come to you eventually. ... For some it takes longer than others."[10]

Dostoyevsky addresses a similar question in *The Brothers Karamazov*. A woman comes to Father Zossima and says, "What if I've been believing all my life, and when I come to die, there's nothing but weeds growing on my grave? I read that in a book. It's awful! How—how can I get back my faith? I only believed when I was a little child mechanically, without thinking of anything. How, how is one to prove it?"

Father Zossima says to her, "There's no proving it, though you can be convinced of it."

"How?" she asks.

Father Zossima replies, "By the experience of active love. Strive to love your neighbor actively and constantly. In so far as you advance in love you will grow surer of the reality of God and of the immortality of your soul."[11]

I agree with Father Zossima. The challenge of loving people has on numerous occasions driven me closer to God. I am not sure I could have survived nearly 40 years of ministry, let alone the other challenges of life, if I had not felt that God was listening to me and sympathizing with me when I felt frustrated, while also encouraging me not to give up.

Acting Our Way into Our Convictions

In the musical *My Fair Lady*, Henry Higgins, a speech teacher, accepts the challenge of taking a poor uneducated girl from the streets of London and transforming her into a high society debutante—a woman of such refinement and sophistication that none of the elite of London would ever guess her true origin. In the case of Eliza Doolittle he begins not with her hair style, clothes, or manners, but with her habits of speech.

This turns out to be the hardest thing for her to change. She practices and practices, but it doesn't help, until suddenly one day she says with clear, beautiful pronunciation, "The rain in Spain stays mainly in the plain." Professor Higgins jerks his head toward her and says, "What did you say?" Without a trace of Cockney accent she says it again: "The rain in Spain stays mainly in the plain." Higgins leaps us and says, "By George, I think she's got it," and they practice saying and singing the words over and over.

It reminds me of what the apostle Paul says in his letter to the Colossians (this time quoting from the older Revised Standard Version Bible):

> Put on then, as God's chosen ones, holy and beloved,
> compassion, kindness, lowliness, meekness, and
> patience, forbearing one another and, if one has a
> complaint against another, forgiving each other; as
> the Lord has forgiven you, so you also must forgive.
> And above all these put on love, which binds
> everything together in perfect harmony (Colossians
> 3:12-14, RSV).

In a sense the Christian faith is a put-on. It involves
putting on the qualities of new life in Christ, even before you
are comfortable with them. It means taking on the character
of Jesus, even before you fully understand or believe who he
is. The disciples did this as they followed Jesus even before
understanding him.

Some people call this hypocrisy, but I call it rehearsing.
People sometimes resent the fact that Christians put on a
show of being nice to each other on Sundays, while the rest
of the week treating people badly. But there is another way
to look at this. On Sundays Christians are rehearsing. Much
of the time they do not yet have the hang of it, and few
have figured out how to do it on Monday through Saturday.
But that is not an argument against practicing our faith on
Sundays. It is an argument for more practice. Hypocrites do
not need less church; they need more. Because the more they
practice a relationship with God, and the more they practice
loving other people, even if it is only one day a week, the
better chance they have of finally getting it.

We can do this because God, in a sense, has already given
us the costumes for our part. We call that justification. Through
Jesus, God has put on us the garments of righteousness that
we did not possess on our own. It may take us a while to
get used to them and learn how to function in them, but the
more we practice the better at it we will get.

In the musical *My Fair Lady* an interesting change
happens in Eliza Doolittle. At the beginning of the movie
Professor Higgins treats her with contempt. He is, after all, a
professor, while she is a tramp. But by the end of the movie
she will not tolerate this anymore. She has spent so much

time practicing dignity, she begins to have dignity. She has rehearsed for so long at being a lady of sophistication and grace, she actually becomes one.

That is the hope of the Christian life. If we keep dressing up as followers of Christ, the clothes may one day begin to fit. If we keep talking to other people like followers of Christ, we may one day begin to change our whole manner of speech. If we practice the demeanor, the attitude, and even the manners of a follower of Christ—even if we repeatedly mess up—one day God may be able to say to us, "I think you've got it."

An Unscientific Postscript

In the movie *Contact* Jodie Foster plays Dr. Ellie Arroway, an astronomer using large arrays of radio telescopes to listen for transmissions from intelligent life in distant galaxies. She is befriended by Palmer Joss, an ex-priest played by Matthew McConaughey. Early in the movie they attend a dinner party at which they begin a running conversation about science and God.

> Ellie: What's more likely: an all-powerful God created the universe and then decided not to give proof of his existence, or that he does not exist at all, and that we created him so we wouldn't have to feel so small and alone?
>
> Palmer: I don't know. I couldn't imagine living in a world where God doesn't exist. I wouldn't want to.
>
> Ellie: How do you know you are not deluding yourself? For me, I'd need proof.
>
> Palmer: Proof. (Pause) Did you love your father?
>
> Ellie: Yes, very much.
>
> Palmer: Prove it.

Faith, like love, is not something you can prove. It is a commitment on which you base your life and which changes your life precisely because you have made the commitment.

I think of a man at the church I served in Spokane, a retired professor of electrical engineering. He was the kind of person who liked things explained, who wanted proof of how things work. For a long time he had trouble with the Christian faith, because many things in the Christian faith are not easily explained, let alone proven. How do you explain the idea that Jesus' death on the cross means our sins are forgiven? It makes no sense. How does Jesus' unjust death make up for the injustice experienced by everyone else? And how do you prove Jesus' resurrection? Science deals with repeatable events. A scientific experiment proves something only if the experiment can be repeated and get the same results. But Jesus' resurrection is an unrepeatable event. Other people may have come back from near-death experiences, but eventually they die again. Jesus conquered death once and for all. How do you prove that? And how do you prove that Jesus' resurrection means that one day we can be raised from the dead to be with him? That also will be an unrepeatable event.

So my engineer friend had trouble believing this stuff. But then he got together with a widow in our church. They were high school sweethearts back in the early 1950s. But after high school, they went their separate ways. Each got married, raised a family, and eventually were widowed. They got reacquainted in 1996. She was a long-time member of our church, and when they got married she asked him to promise that he would bring her to church when it snowed. So he did. At first he came only on the Sundays it snowed. Then one spring I noticed that the snow was gone but he was still bringing her to church. When she signed up to be a host for one of our new member classes, he drove her and decided to stay for the class. He attended several of our new member classes that way. He also attended other classes, and one day he decided to join the church.

I asked him why. He said he had been looking into the Christian faith and had learned a lot. I asked if all his questions were answered, and he said no. But then he said, "I don't need all my questions answered." He explained it this way:

> I know all about how a light switch works. I know how electricity is generated, how it flows through circuits, and how it lights the element in a light bulb. I can explain the whole process. My wife knows none of that. She can't explain anything about how a light bulb works. But she goes through life happily turning on light switches.

> I have learned a lot about the Christian faith from being in classes with people at the church. And I have seen what following Jesus has done for my wife, how strongly she has held on to her faith through difficult times. I may not understand everything about it, but I want to be someone like her who goes through life turning on the lights.

Later in the movie *Contact*, Ellie Arroway picks up radio signals from deep space, not the random noise of the universe, but the clear rhythmic patterns of a purposeful transmission. Eventually these radio signals are decoded and found to contain complete drawings for making a space craft capable of traveling to a remote part of the universe and making contact with the senders of the transmission. So NASA builds the space ship, and Ellie is chosen to fly it. She makes the trip, but because the travel involves a time warp, it appears that she never left. From the point of view of observers on earth she is gone for no length of time and has no proof that she went anywhere. But she did go somewhere, and for her it was a life-changing experience.

Near the end of the movie she is summoned to testify about her trip before a committee of Congress. But when she tries to describe her experience to the committee, she is stymied because she has no proof, no evidence, nothing that can be measured. A counsel of the committee accuses her of being deluded, and the committee chair says to her, "Are we supposed to take all this on faith?" In response she says,

I had an experience. I can't prove it, I can't even explain it, but everything I know as a human being, everything I am tells me it is real. I was given something wonderful, something that changed me forever: a vision of the universe that tells us how undeniably tiny and insignificant and how rare and precious we all are, a vision that tells us we belong to something greater than ourselves, that none of us is alone. I wish I could share that; I wish that everyone even for a moment could feel that awe and humility and hope.

That is what I wish in this book, not that I have proven to you the truth of the Christian faith, but that I have given you a reason to try it and invite others to try it. Another pastor once said to me, "Commitment to Jesus looks like this: Lord, I commit as much of myself as I can to as much of you as I understand. Accept me as I am, and bring me to the place where you want me to be. Amen."

The life of faith begins not with certainty but with a step—a willingness to try embracing the good news revealed by God in Jesus:

- That we are tiny and insignificant, yet rare and precious,
- That we are not alone, and that we belong to Someone greater than ourselves,
- That our past no longer determines our future,
- That the things we do to serve God in this life will never be wasted or forgotten,
- That our lives will one day be caught up into the redeemed creation that God intended for us all along.

My wish is that every one of you could feel that awe and humility and hope.

Questions for Discussion

1. What experiences or questions have posed for you the greatest challenge to believing the Christian faith? How have you dealt with those questions or challenges?

2. What role have the "practices" of faith—worship, prayer, Bible study, being part of a Christian community—had in shaping your faith? Or conversely what has been the effect of the absence of those things from your life?

3. In what way is your faith chosen, and in what way was it given to you? What role did your decisions have in shaping your beliefs? What role was played by things that happened to you or experiences with people whom you met?

4. How would you describe your core beliefs in a series of statements? How would you describe the effect of those beliefs on your life?

Notes

Introduction: *Choosing Faith*

1. Martin Luther, "The Large Catechism" in *The Book of Concord: The Confessions of the Evangelical Lutheran Church*, translated and edited by Theodore G. Tappert (Philadelphia: Fortress Press, 1959): 365.
2. Friedrich Nietzsche, *Thus Spoke Zarathustra*, in *The Portable Nietzsche*, translated by Walter Kaufmann (New York: The Viking Press, 1954): 125. (Author's emphasis)
3. Nietzsche: 219–222.
4. Nietzsche: 366–367.
5. Ted Thornhill, *Daily Mail Online*, January 17, 2014.
6. C. S. Lewis, *The Silver Chair* (New York: Collier Books, 1970): 151–156.
7. C. S. Lewis, *The Silver Chair*: 158–159.
8. Simone Weil, *Waiting for God*, translated by Emma Craufurd (New York: G. P. Putnam's Sons, 1951):210.
9. Yann Martel, *Life of Pi* (Orlando, FL: Harcourt, Inc., 2001): 28.
10. Stephen Hawking and Leonard Mlodinow, *The Grand Design* (New York: Bantam Books, 2010): 165.

Chapter 1: It's Personal

1. See the extensive discussion of these verses, including the history of their interpretation, in Claus Westermann, *Genesis 1-11*, translated by John J. Scullion (Minneapolis: Fortress Press, 1994), 147–158.
2. Westermann: 158.
3. Augustine, *Confessions*, translated by R. S. Pine-Coffin (Middlesex, England: Penguin Books, 1961): 21.
4. "The Shorter Catechism" in *The Constitution of the Presbyterian Church (USA), Part I: Book of Confessions* (Louisville, KY: The Office of the General Assembly, 2014): 205.

5. Karen Armstrong, *A History of God: The 4,000 Year Quest of Judaism, Christianity, and Islam* (New York: Ballantine Books, 1993): 42.
6. Armstrong: 209–210.
7. Robert Coles, *The Spiritual Life of Children* (Boston: Houghton Mifflin Company, 1990): 44.
8. Coles: 44–45.
9. Coles: 45.
10. Described by Jack Rogers in *Presbyterian Creeds: A Guide to the Book of Confessions* (Philadelphia: The Westminster Press, 1985): 185–186.
11. For an example of reading the Bible as a whole, see my book *The Bible's Plot: Connecting the Bible's Story to Your Story* (St. Louis, MO: Lucas Park Books, 2009).
12. Mark Twain, *Huckleberry Finn* (New York: Collier and Son, 1912): 15.
13. Frederick Buechner, *Wishful Thinking: A Theological ABC* (New York: Harper and Row, 1973): 71.
14. The Greek manuscripts of the New Testament differ at this point, some including the words "treat me as one of your hired servants." In this case, however, I think it likely that these words were added to later manuscripts to make them consistent with what the son had planned to say to his father. As Jesus told the story, I think the father cut off the son's carefully prepared speech before he had a chance to bargain.

Chapter 2: What's Wrong with Us?

1. C. S. Lewis, *Mere Christianity* (New York: Collier Books, 1952): 17.
2. Fyodor Dostoyevsky, *The Brothers Karamazov*, translated by Constance Garnett (New York: Signet Books, 1957): 538.
3. David Brooks, "Guilt, Victimhood, and Moral Indignation" (New York Times News Service, 2017). Quoted in *The Seattle Times*, April 2, 2017.
4. Quoted in *Time*, February 27–March 6, 2017: 104.
5. "So the serpent holds out less the prospect of an extension of the capacity for knowledge than the independence that enables a man to decide for himself what will help or hinder him. … God had provided what was good for man (2:18!), and had given him complete security. But now man will go beyond this to decide for himself." Gerhard von Rad, *Genesis: A Commentary*, translated by John Marks (Philadelphia: The Westminster Press, 1972): 60.

6. Robert Bellah, Richard Madsen, William M. Sullivan, Ann Swindler, and Steven M. Tipton, *Habits of the Heart: Individualism and Commitment in American Life* (Berkeley, CA: University of California Press, 1985): 221.
7. For a transcript of the show see Bill Moyers, *Genesis: A Living Conversation* (New York: Doubleday, 1996). The conversation about Noah and the Flood is found on pages 111–153.
8. Moyers: 115.
9. Moyers: 115.
10. Plato, "Phaedo," in *Classics of Western Thought: The Ancient World*, edited by Stebelton H. Nulle (New York: Harcourt, Brace, and World, 1964): 102–103.

Chapter 3: Fixes That Have Not Worked

1. Lesslie Newbigin, *Foolishness to the Greeks: the Gospel and Western Culture* (Grand Rapids, MI: William B. Eerdmans Publishing Company, 1986): 125–126.
2. Aleksandr I. Solzhenitsyn, *The Gulag Archipelago: An Experiment in Literary Investigation, I–II*, translated by Thomas P. Whitney (New York: Harper and Row, 1973): 168.
3. M. Scott Peck, *People of the Lie: The Hope for Healing Human Evil* (NY: Touchstone/Simon and Schuster, 1983): 72.
4. C. S. Lewis, *God in the Dock: Essays on Theology and Ethics*, edited by Walter Hooper (Grand Rapids, MI: William B. Eerdmans Publishing Company, 1970): 153.
5. G. K. Chesterton, *Orthodoxy* (Garden City, NY: Doubleday and Company, 1959): 15.

Chapter 4: Divine Intervention

1. William Sloan Coffin, *Credo* (Louisville, KY: Westminster John Knox Press, 2004): 12.
2. Nikita Stewart and Richard Perez-Pena, "I forgive you, my family forgives you," *The Seattle Times*, June 20, 2015: A-2 and A-5.
3. Dostoyevsky: 222–223.
4. Elie Wiesel, *Night*, translated by Marion Wiesel (NY: Hill and Wang, 1958): 64–65.
5. C. S. Lewis, *Mere Christianity*: 43.
6. *The Qur'an*, translated by M. A. S. Abdel Haleem (Oxford: Oxford University Press, 2004): 65.

Chapter 5: Grace, Relationship, and Transformation

1. Kenneth Bailey identifies this as a key component of the concept "hired hand." "Now he will make up for what he has lost. In short he will save himself. He wants no grace." Kenneth Bailey, *Poet and Peasant and Through Peasant Eyes*, (Grand Rapids, MI: William B. Eerdmans Publishing Company, 1983): 177.
2. Bailey: 194–196.
3. Unpublished poem shared for use by the author.
4. *Book of Confessions*: 58.
5. Martin Luther, "The Small Catechism" in *The Book of Concord: The Confessions of the Evangelical Lutheran Church*, translated and edited by Theodore G. Tappert (Philadelphia: Fortress Press, 1959): 342–344.
6. Fred Craddock, *Craddock Stories*, edited by Mike Graves and Richard F. Ward (St. Louis, MO: Chalice Press, 2001): 156–157.

Chapter 6: Where is the Kingdom?

1. Philip Yancey, *The Bible Jesus Read* (Grand Rapids, MI: Zondervan, 1999): 213.
2. "The present period of the Church is the time between the decisive battle, which has already occurred, and the 'Victory Day.'" Oscar Cullman, *Christ and Time: the Primitive Christian Conception of Time and History*, translated by Floyd V. Filson (Philadelphia: The Westminster Press, 1950): 145.
3. Lesslie Newbegin: 117.
4. Article by Benjamin Weir, *Mission Yearbook of Prayer and Study* (Louisville, KY: Presbyterian Publishing House, 1984).

Chapter 7: The Flawed Representatives of a New Creation

1. *Presbyterian Survey* (July/August, 1987).
2. David Kinnamon and Gabe Lyons, *UnChristian: What a New Generation Really Thinks about Christianity...And Why It Matters* (Grand Rapids, MI: Baker Books, 2007): 72.
3. Christopher Hitchens, *God Is Not Great: How Religion Poisons Everything* (New York: Twelve, Hachette Book Group, 2007): 18.
4. C. S. Lewis, *Mere Christianity*: 177–178.
5. Rodney Stark, *The Rise of Christianity* (San Francisco, CA: Harper Collins, 1997): 5–6.
6. Stark: 161.
7. C. S. Lewis, *God in the Dock*: 61–62.

8. Though widely attributed to Pascal, I have not been able to find a written source for this quotation. Whatever its source it carries a deep insight.
9. Like the above quotation from Pascal, I have not been able to find a written source for this quotation, but it has deep meaning for Christian life, whatever its source.

Chapter 8: Revisiting the Problem of Evil

1. Rob Bell, *Love Wins: A Book about Heaven, Hell, and the Fate of Every Person Who Ever Lived* (New York: Harper One, 2011): 36–38.
2. Newbegin: 136.
3. King Josiah "defiled" the valley of Hinnom as part of his reform measures to eradicate the worship of gods by child sacrifice (II Kings 23:10). This means he made it a place where waste considered ritually unclean could be dumped. Hence its status in the New Testament as a garbage dump. James R. Edwards, *The Gospel According to Mark* (Grand Rapids, Mil: William B. Eerdmans, 2002): 294–295.
4. "Satan's loss of access to the heavenly court means that no further accusations can be brought against the faithful. They are safe from the threat of further indictments in the heavenly court." Adela Yarbro Collins, *The Combat Myth in the Book of Revelation* (Eugene, OR: Wipf and Stock Publishers, 2001):141.
5. Jonathan Kozol, *Amazing Grace: The Lives of Children and the Conscience of a Nation* (New York: Harper Collins, 1995): 84.
6. Kozol: 237–238.

Chapter 9: Hope and Courage

1. Jurgen Moltmann, *In the End—the Beginning: the Life of Hope*, translated by Margaret Kohl (Minneapolis, MN: Fortress Press, 2004): 87–88. (Author's emphasis)
2. Leslie McKenna, *"Lament of a Seed"* unpublished poem. Used by permission.
3. Karle Wilson Baker, "Courage," in *Poetry: A Magazine of Verse* (Oct., 1921): 16.
4. Cyril C. Richardson, editor, *Early Christian Fathers* (New York: Simon and Schuster, 1996): 152, 154.
5. Patricia Wilson-Kastner, G. Ronald Kastner, Ann Millin, Rosemary Rader, and Jeremiah Reedy, *A Lost Tradition: Women*

Writers of the Early Church (Lanham, MD: University Press of America, 1981): 20, 22.

6. Harriet Beecher Stowe, *Uncle Tom's Cabin* (New York: Signet Classic, 1998): 386–387, 412 (author's emphasis).

7. Corrie ten Boom with John and Elizabeth Sherrill, *The Hiding Place* (Minneapolis, MN: A Chosen Book, 1971): 179.

Chapter 10: How to Believe

1. Christian Smith, with Melinda Lundquist Denton, *"Soul Searching: the Religious and Spiritual Lives of American Teenagers* (New York: Oxford University Press, 2005): 17–20.

2. Donald Miller, *Blue Like Jazz: Nonreligious Thoughts on Christian Spirituality* (Nashville, TN: Thomas Nelson, 2003): 51.

3. Miller: 52–53.

4. Philip Yancey, *Reaching for the Invisible God* (Grand Rapids, MI: Zondervan Publishing House, 2000): 65–66.

5. Blaise Pascal, *Pensées*, translated by A. J. Krailsheimer (London: Penguin Books, 1966): 151.

6. Pascal: 153.

7. Miller: 58.

8. C. S. Lewis, *Surprised by Joy: The Shape of My Early Life* (Orlando, FL: Harcourt, Inc., 1955): 224.

9. Pascal: 274.

10. Kathleen Norris, *Amazing Grace: a Vocabulary of Faith* (New York: Riverhead Books, 1998): 64–65.

11. Dostoyevsky: 60.